The Breakup Repair Kit

Marni Kamins and Janice MacLeod

CONARI PRESS

First published in 2004 by Conari Press, an imprint of
Red Wheel/Weiser, LLC York Beach, ME

With offices at: 368 Congress Street, Boston, MA 02210

www.redwheelweiser.com

Library of Congress Cataloging-in-Publication Data
Kamins, Marni.
The breakup repair kit / Marni Kamins and Janice MacLeod.
p. cm.
ISBN 1-57324-919-X
1. Man–woman relationships. 2. Separation (Psychology)
3. Single women—Psychology. I. MacLeod, Janice. II. Title.
HQ801.K325 2004
306.7—dc22

2003015685

Typeset in Bembo
Printed in the United States of America
RRD

The paper used in this publication meets the minimum requirements of
the American National Standard for Information Sciences-Permanence
of Paper for Printed Library Materials Z39.48-1992 (R1997).

11 10 09 08 07 06 05 04   8 7 6 5 4 3 2

For all those who have fallen in,
crawled out, and stood again.

Contents

Foreword

Ow, Ow, Ow, Ow, Ow, Ow, *Ow!*

I know! It hurts. It really, really hurts. Whether you are the dump-ee or the dump-er, a breakup hurts. Of course it does. And it should. Not because you're a bad person, but because . . . well, let's put it this way: God forbid you should date someone you wouldn't miss! It's also normal for you to have mixed feelings about a breakup, as in "I never want to see you again . . . unless you're wearing those jeans!" or "Wow, you're cute when you're packing." It all goes with the tricky, murky, yucky territory.

Still, all of this is—in terms of your ultimate happiness and loveability—just the messy stuff of life, not the sloppy kiss of death. In fact, here's the good news you'll find in this book: You'll be over it before you know it. Know why? Because "over it" doesn't mean that you never think of him, or that it doesn't hurt when you do. "Over it" means that there might still be a little piece of him stuck to your back, in that place you can't reach. But hey, it's on your back, not in your way. You, Miss Thing, are free to move on. And that's just what Marni and Janice's *Breakup Repair Kit* will do: help you move on while holding on to everything you will have learned about yourself and about what you'll need from your next relationship. Which brings me to the other good news. Now you're free to meet *The One!*

—Lynn Harris, co-creator of *BreakupGirl.net*

Heard you broke up . . .

Congratulations!

The very fact that you have opened this book means that you have begun to heal. You are showing yourself that you are willing to learn from your experiences. Nice job! You deserve an amazing, wonderful, and juicy life.

With love,
Janice and Marni

ntroduction

We have both been through intense breakups, and we have come out the other end feeling better. This book holds comforting tools to keep you company through your breakup, the aftermath, and then the next relationship.

In Part I, "The Mourning After," you will be introduced to the various stages of healing. We will show you how to deal with what is coming up and how to counsel yourself as you go through the stages of loss.

In Part II, "Rebuild Your Life," you will learn what you want to do with all the extra time you now have without him. We help you remember what you once loved, how to nurture your relationship with yourself, and how rebuild your life.

In Part III, "Back in the Saddle," we help you experiment with getting back into the dating scene and knowing when you are ready to start. We offer tips and advice on how to love yourself as you pass into the next phase of your life.

Be bold, be brave, and continue on!

About the Authors . . . Breakups

Janice's Breakup

My most painful breakup was (and is) hard to get over. We broke up at the beginning of summer. He says it was mutual. It wasn't. I sensed he wanted out, so we decided to break up. The summer was a blur for me. My head was cloudy, and I couldn't think clearly. I know I probably cried a lot, read a lot, and felt really yucky most of the time. But I can't really remember the summer season. It's like my brain shut off so that I could focus on trying to live my life as normally as I could. For months, I didn't tell anyone we had broken up. Whenever someone would ask about him, I'd simply say he was working a lot and was fine. They figured no news was good news.

I couldn't speak the words "we broke up" without crying. Autumn came, and the cold snap snapped me out of my brain haze. I fell apart. I began to cry and get angry. I was having a hard time dealing. But with advice from friends, professional help, and time, it's starting to ease up.

Breakups teach. There are lessons to learn from every relationship. Sometimes it takes a long time to learn what those lessons are. Keep the faith. If you want healing, you'll get it exactly when you need it. And you'll be better off for it.

—Janice

Marni's Breakup

The sadness after my breakup felt confusing because I was the one who initiated the breakup. I thought he was my first love. I thought he was the one I had been waiting for my whole life. Not staying with him felt like it would be the mistake of my life. He told me we might be soul mates—something I had always dreamed of. He had everything that I thought was important, and he seemed so much more grown up than I was. I thought that if I were with him, I would learn how to be more like him. He was so fearless and persistent in taking me out. No one had ever cared that much about getting to know me. I didn't want to let go of him and run the risk of regretting it for the rest of my life.

But I also couldn't ignore how drained I felt when I spent time with him. And how unheard, unseen, and alone I felt when we were intimate. I felt like my wings were clipped. I figured this was as good as it gets so I'd better settle in for the long run. He was a wonderful, sweet, gentle man who I thought treated me well. Still, I felt caged and not good enough. I could never seem to give him what he wanted from me. I thought that maybe we would get married, that he would save me and make my life okay and comfortable. I thought he would hand me success. But I wasn't happy. I felt tired and used up. So I broke up. It was heartbreaking and wonderful. I felt sad and hurt and especially guilty about putting my happiness first by deciding to break up. There was a new freedom in going to sleep in fresh sheets and waking up rested. My life felt less crowded and lighter all of the sudden. I started to enjoy the little things; for instance, it felt delicious to eat food that gave me bad breath because I knew I wouldn't be kissing him that day. I felt like my wings were growing back.

—Marni

Part One

The Mourning After

The most painful part of a breakup is usually at the beginning. Take comfort in knowing that what you are going through now is probably the worst of it. Whew. That's good news. In studying the art of loss, one truth is always woven throughout everyone's experience. When something happens in our lives that we don't want to happen—whether it comes as a shock or we have spent months preparing for it—we all inevitably do the same thing first. We push it away. Rich people, poor people, perfect-looking people, movie stars, famous clothing designers, everyone. The unavoidable first instinct of us all is to push away what we didn't want to happen.

So if you want to push away everything you are feeling, we don't blame you; breakups are no fun. However, the deeper your pain, especially if you dare to feel it, the deeper your pleasure will be when you come out the other side. If you are willing to feel the uncomfortable feelings and sit with them, rich rewards will await you as the feelings pass. You will always get exactly what you give. If you give yourself this time to heal, you'll be rewarded with a richer, fuller life than you ever thought imaginable.

Denying the Truth Feels Good...at First

Right now if you are in a state of mourning, and you are pushing away your feelings, they will not go away. If you do not deal with the breakup, your emotions will intensify and seep into your everyday life when you least expect it.

Remember, it is natural to want to push away what we don't want to feel; however, when we continue to resist, we are doing something called denying reality. How do you know if you are denying reality? You feel it because everything in your life seems heavier. Everything you do—waking up in the morning, going to work, taking care of yourself—everything is incredibly difficult. You feel like anything could push you over the edge. You feel like you are white knuckling yourself through all your days. Going about life like this feels dull and tiring. The best thing you can do is deal with your hurt, anger, confusion, and so forth head on so that you can get over it already.

How to "Get over It Already"

Easier said than done. Luckily there is light at the end of the tunnel. You can choose to settle into what you are feeling, thereby allowing it to pass. Thank goodness, because feeling it is actually very simple. First, ask yourself what is going on in your body and what you are feeling that you want so badly to ignore. Allow whatever is going on in your body to present itself. Don't feel that you have to come up with concrete answers. Then ask yourself if those feelings are feelings you are willing to feel—just for right now. They don't have to be pleasant, and you can want to change them. Ask yourself if you can let go of the desire to change what is happening and let it be okay just for today. That is all you have to do. Settle into your feelings and allow them space to expand. They will pass; we promise.

We live in such an analytical culture that it is easy to get stuck trying to figure ourselves out. We are easily tricked into not feeling by trying so hard to figure out why. For right now, let everything be okay, no need to figure out the meaning. Simply allow yourself to mourn.

The
Mourning
After

11

What to
Expect
When
You're
Healing

The process of healing can be wonderful . . . like the feeling after a really good pee. So satisfying. As you heal from your breakup, you will develop useful tools you will have for the rest of your life.

The Eight Stages of Healing After a Breakup

These grieving stages are normal parts of the healing process. The healthiest thing for you to do is to let them run their course rather than using your energy to try to fight them off. (Or, if you want, you can ignore all your feelings, push them away, keep dating the same type of loser over and over, and sit in your own crap. Your choice.)

Also be aware that these stages do not always happen in sequence. Do not be disturbed if you start out in Stage 4 and go into Stage 1. Be prepared for the stages to feel as if they are not happening fast enough. By allowing them to follow their course, you will ensure an easy return to the way your life was before he strolled into town.

Stage 1: Shock

You feel disbelief. Your mind is deciding to deny your pain because it is too painful to process the truth. It is normal to experience excessive fantasizing and the belief that nothing is wrong. You think, "What the . . . ? Are we really not together anymore? Am I sure? Maybe it was all a dream. Maybe he's really left for a season, and I will go into the bathroom to see him showering." Or, "Maybe it just hasn't hit me yet. It's funny how I feel so fine with all this. After two years with someone, I am not even that phased." *What should you do?* Nothing. Feel the shock. Don't make any major changes. Find yourself a good listener, not an advice giver, and talk about it.

Stage 2: Denial

You completely deny the loss. You don't even feel sad. You want to wake up and have it be over. You think, "Wait, we had so many plans. I seriously think that we were meant to be together. What about our future, are all those dreams just *cancelled*? It can't *really* be over. Deep down I know that we're just on a break. I trust that we are soul mates, and this time apart will actually turn out to be good for us. I saw my future when I gazed into his eyes. What about that dream beach house that we talked about? How

could I be wrong? The giggling. The spooning." This is where you torture yourself because it feels good—like playing with a loose tooth or overusing tweezers. You also go into bargaining when you think, "If only I had done this," or "had waited to say that," then all this never would have happened. Bargaining is normal and you will eventually stop. *What should you do with denial?* Realizing you are in denial is enough. Being conscious of your denial is a giant step forward. Wait until it passes.

Stage 3: Numbness

You think to yourself, "I am so surprised at how easy he was to get over. I'm not even crying. Too bad for him. In fact, nothing in my whole life seems to matter anymore. I am not hungry or passionate about anything. Is there supposed to be some kind of grand purpose in life? If there is, who cares? I am not even horny. I could care less if I ever date again." *What should you do?* The numb period will pass when you are ready. Your mind is protecting you from what feels overwhelming.

Stage 4: Fear

Fear is rooted in a delusion; it is extreme thinking, and none of it is based on fact. Fearful thinking is all self-manufactured and delusional. "What if I'll never date again? Was he as good as it gets? I'll never get married. I'll never have children. I'll end my days alone in a dusty old house knitting booties for the children I wish I had." *What should you do with fear?* Fear is necessary because it is part of the healing process, but the sooner you remind yourself that the fearful thoughts are not true, the stronger you will feel about moving on. It is helpful to talk about your fears with a nonjudgmental friend who will remind you that those thoughts are not true facts.

Stage 5: Anger

Anger is good. Unexpressed, repressed anger is bad. You may find yourself thinking, "Wait a minute. We never did any of those things we said we were going to do. He never came through on any of his promises. It was all talk! What a schmuck. It's all his fault. I can't believe I was stupid enough to love such a low-life hairy ball of earwax." *What should you do?* Let your anger out in healthy ways. Have some good revenge fantasies. Hate his guts if it makes you feel better.

However, be careful not to get too caught up here. Anger can make you bitter. Listen to your gut. If your anger feels unsurmountable, seek help until it passes.

Stage 6: Depression

"I have no one to go to brunch with anymore. And even if I did, I'd rather stay in my bed and eat Tootsie Rolls. I have no life. I loathe myself. I wish I were pretty and skinny and rich. Then I would be happy." It is common to lose the hope that our lives will ever return to the peace and order we felt before. The truth is that our lives will return to normal and every thing will be fine. *What should you do?* Allow yourself to feel the despair. If the despair makes you feel suicidal or is unbearable, don't wait to get professional help. Get it now.

Stage 7: Understanding

"I learned so much from dating him. And I'm really glad I'm not dating him anymore. I guess we were not supposed to be together and that's okay." In this stage, you begin to reach a level of awareness and understanding, and see the truth for the first time. You see that maybe it wasn't meant to be. You may not quite yet be grateful that you broke up, but you are starting to see that you will have a wonderful, rich life without him.

Stage 8: Acceptance

"He was not perfect, but neither was I. We were meant to be together for the time that we were together. I learned from him and he learned from me; I feel pretty complete with the circle that was our relationship. Now, bring on the other fish in the sea. I'm fabulous."

Janice's Stage of Healing at this Moment

For months following a particular nasty moment I had with my ex-boyfriend, I'd been depressed. During my depression, I missed him terribly. Then, he called for the first time since our falling out. After the phone call, I had to put my head between my knees because I had so many emotions well up in me that my body couldn't handle it. It wasn't anything he said; it was just because he had called and I had to hear his voice again. The feeling soon passed, and for a few days afterward, I felt lightheaded and numb. I was surprised at how aloof I was about our conversation. Then I snapped out of the numbness and felt anger. For days, I was angry with him for calling, for his not getting his life together, and especially at myself for not seeing him for who he really was. My body was tense, I couldn't sleep, and I didn't even have the energy to go for a walk. After a week had gone by, I found myself crying easily. Sad commercials made me cry. Being caught in traffic made me cry. Being slightly embarrassed, angry, tense, tired, or annoyed made me cry. Yet at the same time, I still went out with friends, laughed, and enjoyed myself. But one night I went to a movie, and it was about 45 minutes too long for me. When the movie finally finished, I was angry that the director hadn't thought to cut down the movie. Of course, my anger wasn't about the director. It was about me. I know I should have let myself ride through this time and experience all my emotions. Easier said than done. Now, when I'm feeling these intense emotions, I don't attempt to understand why. I wait until later, when my body has calmed down, to review why I was so angry or sad or whatever. So, just in the past few weeks I went from numbness to anger to depression, and back to anger. I look forward to the day I'm over it all. I've been told that time heals. Seems to be taking forever. We'll see. I'll let you know.

Time Heals All

Your psyche knows that this is the process you will go through, even if you don't consciously know what it's doing. Going through these stages is not up to you. It will happen naturally, and whatever sequence it happens in is the best sequence for you. As you take care of your physical and spiritual self, trust that your brain will take care of your mental and emotional self. You know instinctively how to get back into balance. Give yourself time to heal. It could take minutes or it could take years, depending on

how deep the relationship was. You are a wise person. You innately know what is best for you. Listen to your instincts. During some of these stages, especially the depression stage, you may think that it's never going to end. It will. The process of emotional healing has a definite beginning, middle, and end. This too shall pass. Remind yourself of this often. What you are going through is normal. And it is going to be okay.

Snakes and Ladders Healing

The eight stages of healing are just that—stages. They aren't steps. Healing is not like walking up stairs. Healing is like playing a game of Snakes and Ladders. You walk up a few steps, land on a snake and slide down a few steps. You climb again and maybe fall again. Just when you feel you're making headway, you could fall back and not understand why. While you're in this Snakes and Ladders healing, realize that the healing process is doing its job. We experience a gamut of feelings as we grow. We can be patient with ourselves during this time, or we can choose to be angry, judgmental, and beat ourselves up mercilessly. It's best to just give ourselves a break when getting over a breakup.

Nurture Nest

I mmediately following your breakup, make a nurture nest for yourself and let yourself stay home. The earliest nurture nests were those forts you made out of blankets and chairs when you were a kid. It was a whole other world inside that fort. A private, dark, and warm cave where you were the master of your own domain. Inside a nurture nest, you can hear silence and let your inner monologue speak. If you listen hard, you might hear spirits whispering secrets.

In a nurture nest, you are your own mom and get to take good care of yourself.

Nurture Nests Are Magic Healing Spaces

After a breakup, building and spending quality time in a nurture nest is a very healing experience. One of the best ways to hasten the first stage of healing is to lean into the pain and allow yourself to mourn. Embrace your loss. Write about it, think about it, and begin separating yourself from the relationship. Know that what was wrong with the relationship is not wrong with you. During your time in the nurture nest, you'll want to allow yourself to focus on healing your heart.

Though friends may try to cheer you up by taking you out, if you would rather stay home, be okay with holding back and telling them you think it's best to spend some quality time alone. You are not a loser if you stay home on a Saturday night. Au contraire! You are bravely sticking up for yourself. You are daring to seek inside yourself to find your inner voice and ask it where to go from here. Put on some comfy clothes, lock the doors, and feel your feelings. When you allow yourself to feel your feelings, they will pass more quickly. Stay in tonight. Make a nurture nest. Let yourself feel. It may not feel good to feel, but it will help you move on. And don't call him.

It may sound crazy to build a nurture nest. After all, you're a grownup right? Hmm . . . Support yourself. Stop being a grownup, get out the chairs and blankets, and start building.

How to Build Your Nurture Nest
You'll need:

+ Four chairs
+ Three soft blankets
+ Pillows (a plethora of them)
+ A flashlight
+ A journal
+ Inspiring and juicy books and comics
+ Pens and crayons
+ Watercolors

+ Big paper

+ Tea

+ Snacks

+ Music

+ Stuff to pamper yourself with

+ A vibrator (optional)

Building instructions:

1. Set up three or four chairs so the chair seats face outward.

2. Place soft blankets or pillows on the floor in between the chairs. (A sheepskin rug is wonderful for this.)

3. Throw big sheets or blankets over the chairs.

Voila! A perfect nurture nest.

Places for a nurture nest:

+ Under the dining table

+ In the living room

+ On top of your bed (or under it)

Nurture Nest

23

Alternate nurture nests:

+ A tent with a good zipper
+ A bubble bath, complete with candles, soft music, and a locked bathroom door
+ A rented cottage by the sea or a fancy hotel room (how decadent!)

Nurture Nest Activities

The task for you right now is to separate yourself from the loss of your boyfriend. If part of your definition of yourself was as an "us," a breakup may leave you feeling empty, as if part of you doesn't exist anymore. You've lost something, but you still exist. A positive thing to do is replace your loss with a gain. Your goal is to reown yourself. You are no longer one of two people. This can be a freeing (or scary) thought. You are on the precipice of the next phase of your life. How very exciting. The nurture nest helps you bring the focus back to yourself.

POWER TOOL
Take off Your Work Clothes

It's time to relax. One of the easiest and fastest ways to do this is to change into pajamas as soon as you return home. Eat dinner in your pj's. Do laundry in them. You'll be comfy and happy.

RECIPE

Soothing Oatmeal and Honey Facial Mask

1 egg white
1 teaspoon honey
1/4 cup oatmeal

Blend the oatmeal finely in a blender. Mix all ingredients in a bowl. Rub mask all over your face to exfoliate. Leave on for approximately two minutes. Rinse off with warm water.

Yield: One mask.

Pamper yourself

Buy cool pajamas, hair softener, or lavender bath salts. Give yourself a pedicure or manicure. Put a mint mask on your face and cucumber slices over your eyes. The universe will treat you the way you treat yourself, so treat yourself well.

Meditate

Don't worry about not knowing how or being good at it. Meditation is in the doing. Lie on your back with your arms spread out like wings or sit cross-legged with your hands resting comfortably on your knees. Close your eyes and breathe. Concentrate on your breath to clear the thoughts from your head. Let any thoughts that pop up go away. When your mind wanders, go back to your breathing. Meditate for as long as you can. If you think you might lose track of time, you can set an alarm for five minutes, then later for eight minutes, then twenty minutes, and so on. Just focus on your breathing. Breathe in and out, and let your belly remain soft.

Yoga

Yoga unites the mind, body, and spirit by connecting the breath to the body through physical poses. Yoga allows your body to move in unison with your breath. The practice can alleviate stress, muscle aches, menstrual cramps, depression, and even constipation. Yogis use a special yoga mat, which has enough grip to keep you from slipping during the poses. If you don't have a yoga mat, a large towel laid out on the carpet can be a nice alternative. Here are some poses to do for a quick pick-me-up and to alleviate stress.

Brain Booster. This pose sends oxygen to the brain, promoting clarity, serenity, and balance. Connect each movement of the pose with your breathing.

1. Sit cross-legged.

2. Inhale and place your hands over your heart.

Pumpkin Body Mask

RECIPE

2 tablespoons honey
2 tablespoons oatmeal
2 tablespoons cornmeal
1/4 cup pumpkin (you can use the canned variety)
1/2 cup heavy cream

Mix the ingredients together. Stand in the shower to apply. This could get messy. Apply the mask all over your body. The oatmeal and cornmeal exfoliate, while the honey, pumpkin, and cream moisturize. Then rinse in the shower.

3. Exhale and tilt your head gently toward your right shoulder.

4. Inhale and lift your head back to center.

5. Exhale and tilt your head gently toward your left shoulder.

6. Repeat for a minute or two . . . or as long as it feels good.

Calm Creator. This pose gives your spine a loving hug. It not only helps you release knots and tension along your spine, but it also increases blood flow to your brain, thus enhancing creative thinking.

1. Lie on your back with your arms stretched out.

2. Inhale and bend your right knee toward your chest.

3. Exhale and gently fold your right knee over your straight left leg.

4. Turn your head and look at your right hand.

5. Take many breaths. On each exhalation, gently twist further into the pose as far as it feels comfortable.

6. Switch sides and repeat.

More Nurture Nest Activities

The following are more nurture activities.

Write Him a Letter

Write your ex a letter in your journal to tell him how this breakup is making you feel. Here are some ideas:

+ Write him a letter from your inner five-year-old telling him you're going to tell his parents what he did so he'll get in trouble.

+ Write him a letter from your inner bitch telling him what you would do to him if there weren't laws against it.

+ Write him a letter from the hurt girl who just wants his love and doesn't understand why he does what he does.

+ Write him a letter telling him you are mad that he didn't live up to your expectations.

+ Write him a letter of appreciation because of what you learned from the relationship. Tell him how you now know what you no longer want in a partner. Tell him how you are a stronger person now than you were when you were first dating him. Tell him you won't ever take his crap again.

It is important to write in your journal because it helps you realize what you feel. You are the sole proprietor of your journal. Inside your journal, you can write down whatever you want, and you can be as honest as you want. Be mean. Be pathetic. Be sad. Be immature. Spill your guts. Once you've written out everything that is clogging your channels, burn the letters, shred them or tear them up gleefully into a million pieces. Don't read them over and take them back in. Release them.

Weep

This works best when you're lying in the fetal position with a wad of tissues in hand. Get good and snotty. Or bawl directly into a pillow and see how wet you can make it. Then, call someone that you love and trust and cry like Barbie will when she realizes Ken has no package. Cry and let your friend tell you how she never really liked him anyway. Consider going to your parents' house for the weekend to hide out. Then rent a sad movie instead. Here are some real tearjerkers:

+ *Beaches*
+ *My Girl*
+ *City of Angels*
+ *Moulin Rouge*
+ *Titanic*

Cry until you cry yourself dry. Until you're lightheaded and fully tapped out. Then, lie in child's pose (kneel with your knees shoulder width apart, sit on your heels, then bend forward with your forehead on the floor and your arms at your sides). Breathe deeply.

Still More Nurture Nest Activities

At first, it might feel unfamiliar in the nurture nest. You've created this loving space, but you don't know what to do to nurture yourself inside it. Here are a few more activities for when you are in your nurture nest.

POWER TOOL
Self-Support vs. Self-Indulgence

Ever feel like you are being self-indulgent with your feelings? Feel like you are talking too much or crying on too many shoulders? Sometimes what we feel as self-indulgent is really self-support. It just may feel out of place to be taking such loving care of yourself.

Nap

Take a guilt-free nap. Healing can be exhausting. Your body needs to regenerate.

Zone Out

Zoning out after something bad happens is okay. If your head is cloudy, let it be cloudy. If it takes effort to think, don't think. Instead of thinking, "My head is so cloudy, I probably need a cup of coffee," or, "I must need some sugar or a cigarette," just let yourself be unfocused and zone out. Your mind may be creating a wall of protection to help you deal with an overwhelming experience. Zoning out is one way your body gets your mind to sleep. Go with it and zone out.

Read

Shut off the phone, computer, TV, and radio. Hop into your nurture nest with a flashlight and some nurturing literature, such as:

+ *The Giving Tree* by Shel Silverstein
+ *The Artist's Way* by Julia Cameron
+ *The Absolutely Essential Eloise* by Kay Thompson, illustrated by Hilary Knight
+ *Olivia* by Ian Falconer
+ *I Know Why the Caged Bird Sings* by Maya Angelou

+ *Spilling Open* by Sabrina Ward Harrison

+ *Succulent Wild Woman* by SARK

+ *Griffin & Sabine* trilogy by Nick Bantock

+ *O: The Oprah Magazine*

+ *The Tale of the Unknown Island* by José Saramago

+ *Jane* magazine

+ *Good in Bed* by Jennifer Weiner

+ *Many Lives, Many Masters* by Brian L. Weiss

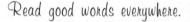

Read good words everywhere.

Black and White Thinking

Breakups can make us think and act a little frantic. The pain of fresh wounds can make us think mean or self-pitying thoughts and engage in erratic, perhaps even psychotic behavior. This kind of delusional thought is called "black and white thinking."

Delusion: (de-loo shun): Something accepted as true that is actually false or unreal. Unsound, misleading reasoning.

Janice and Marni's Black and White Thoughts

"I'm going to be like my old aunt who never got married and never had kids."

"Whom will I go to the farmer's market with? It won't ever be fun again without him."

"I never want to be with anyone else. There is no one like him."

"I'll never find a lover as attentive as he is."

"But he was my soul mate."

"He understood me better than anyone else."

"I'll never find another person whom I feel that comfortable with."

"I'll never have sex again."

"No one is ever going to love me like he loved me. No one will ever sing to me again."

"He's gone because I'm ugly and fat."

"There is no one in the whole world as perfect as him."

Marni's Delusion

I kept thinking that had I been prettier or skinnier, maybe our relationship would have worked out the way I wanted. The thing is, our breakup wasn't about my body or looks. I just wanted to see it that way so I could use our breakup to beat myself up.

I did the very best I could to be honest and present and 100 percent myself. At that point, it was not my business to figure out why our relationship didn't work. I just needed to give myself space to feel my feelings and concentrate on being self-loving.

Worst Case Scenarios

Our delusional thoughts can send us into a tailspin of fear and anxiety. Everything can feel like the worst possible thing that could ever happen. Here are a few common worst case scenarios.

Worst Case Scenario: I'll Never Love Anyone Else as Long as I Live

Right. Like you know that what the future holds. There is always more to be revealed. Would you have really been happy with this dude for the rest of your life? You want someone that craves you exactly as much as you crave him. Try to be realistic; remember all the negative things about him. Go look back at your journals. Remember the bad stuff. When we have a broken heart, we also have selective memory. We seem to only remember the good times and forget that he was a putz. You have been in love before, and you didn't even know it was going to happen; hence, you will be in love again, and it will happen at the most unexpected time.

You're thinking that you will never love again because you are being forced to break the habit of being with him. Dating this fellow was a habit; whether it's a good habit or bad habit, it's still a habit. Good news: habits can be broken. This sudden breakup forces you to go cold turkey, and the craving for his attention can make you feel like you are constantly missing something. When you first fall in love, it may feel like you're being swept away. You're not mistaken. Your newly smitten body is flooded with chemicals like dopamine, norepinephrine, phenylethylamine, and oxytocin. These are comfort chemicals and boy they feel great. One reason it feels so horrible when we've been abandoned is because we don't have our daily hit of these chemicals and we are suffering withdrawal symptoms. We really can be addicted to love. Hence, when we hear his voice or smell his smell, our brains are flooded with these chemicals again and we feel comforted even though it may feel contrary to the way we normally feel about him when he's not around. Remember, this too shall pass. Here are a few quick tips for getting through the initial craving.

+ **Have a bawl fest.** If you feel heartbroken, that is okay. Go ahead and feel that way. Honor your heart's feelings. If you want to, grieve so much that your eyes become red and puffy, your stomach hurts, and you feel as if you just ran a marathon. Bawling releases tons of pent up tension and, believe it or not, can tire your body enough to make it difficult to think too much. Plus, bawling can give you a fabulous night's sleep. And it's good for your complexion.

+ **Have an après bawl fest.** Fill up your calendar with activities, put on your lipstick, and head out the door. Go dancing. Go shopping. Go see whatever movie you want. Flirt with the cute boys in the video store. Invite people out for popcorn, snowcaps, and movie theme nights. Not only will you begin to notice that there are many more, cuter fish in the sea, but also if he should call, you will be out and about, and who knows where.

+ **Don't be a victim.** Don't assume the position of a victim. Seriously now, you are a survivor, not a victim. Whatever went wrong between you and buffoon boy is not a reflection on you as a person. You may feel as if you'll never love again because so much of your life was surrounded by this relationship. Sometimes we make our relationships the pivotal point that our lives revolve around, rather than making ourselves the pivotal point of our lives. Sometimes it feels too selfish to have our lives revolve around ourselves. It's not selfish, it's self-nurturing.

Lesson #1: You must put yourself first. Did you make him your Higher Power? Did you assign him more importance in your life than you should have?

Lesson #2: Everything happens for a reason, and maybe the reason this breakup happened has not yet been revealed. Sometimes our angels do for us what we cannot do for ourselves. Be patient. You'll discover that there are divine reasons why you dated this person and why you broke up. In the meantime, if you don't act like a victim, you won't feel like one.

> **POWER TOOL**
>
> *Just Wait*
>
> *When the moment seems unbearable, remember, this too shall pass.*

Worst Case Scenario: I Have No Money and Nowhere to Go

If you were co-habiting and co-dependent on this fella, you may feel as if you are left with nothing in the world when he packs his bags . . . or packed yours. Ask for help. Write a letter of intent: State your intentions to find your own way and become self-supporting. Send it out to people you know who are in a position to help. Reach out to anyone who will listen. Places of worship are good starting points because either they will have organizations within their worship community that you can turn to or they will know local charitable organizations that can help.

Marni's $7,000 Friend

I have a friend who could not afford to keep paying for school after she broke up with her boyfriend of three years who was paying for her schooling. She was a year away from getting her degree and did not want to drop out. She decided to write a letter of intent stating her plan to finish school and become a teacher. She wrote in the letter that she needed exactly $7,000 more dollars to finish school. She gave a copy of the letter to people who she knew were in a position to help her. She received an anonymous check for $7,000 two weeks later. Miracles do happen if you ask for them and are willing to receive help.

Give First to Receive

You can also do the opposite. Huh? Instead of asking for help, give help. Reach out to someone else, and the universe will see your good intentions and provide for you. Volunteer at a soup kitchen or tutor at a local school. Take animal shelter puppies for walks. They will love your attention, and they just want to love you.

Put your energy into reaching out to the world. Ask your Higher Power for help and accept that you are worthy of receiving assistance.

Worst Case Scenario: I Have No One Left in the Whole Wide World Who Loves Me

You may feel as if you have no one to turn to for comfort because your nighttime, sniffling, whining, sorry-ass, selfish, disrespectful, rude, won't-let-you-get-rest boyfriend was your *everything*. If you feel alone, know that right now you are not alone. Feeling alone is a delusion. Not only do you have yourself, but you also have the constant company of a Higher Power. You do, whether you choose to believe it or not. Developing a relationship with your Higher Power will keep you from feeling lonely. To learn how, read the chapter entitled "Connect With Your Higher Power." You are no more alone now than you were when you were with your ex-boyfriend. *There is a power greater than yourself that will never allow anything into your life that you can't handle.* Everyone feels alone at times. If the fear of being alone seems overwhelming, therapy is an excellent option. A good therapist will listen, be supportive, put things in perspective, and help you distinguish between being alone and being lonely.

POWER TOOL

Ancient Principle

Sometimes things have to get worse before they can get better.

Worst Case Scenario: He Cheated on Me and I Probably Have an STD

Okay, this worst case scenario is kind of a big deal. Immediately go to your doctor to get tested. If you are afraid to go to the doctor, understand that knowledge of what is going on in your body is your best defense. Going to get tested won't make it worse, but not knowing will.

How to Snap out of Your Delusions

When you find yourself engaging in wacky behavior (or a friend informs you that you are), use these tools to get yourself out of your delusional cloud:

+ **Don't make any major changes.** People have been known to do the most outrageous things after a breakup. They go on big expensive trips and engage in elaborate redecorating, tattoos, piercings, drastic haircuts, and so on. We've also been known to make drunken late night phone calls to our exes. Before you act on a major change, stop, breathe, and call a trusted friend who will give you a reality check.

+ **Fake it till you make it.** It's easy to fall into panic mode after a breakup. When you catch yourself using key words like "never again," "no one," and "nothing," remember that you are engaging in black & white thinking and none of it is based on fact. Then, think the opposite, even if it sounds fake. For instance, instead of "I'll *never* love again," say "I will *easily* love again." Eventually, you'll start believing your positive thoughts rather than your delusional thoughts.

+ **Get out of your head.** Stop thinking so much. Start doing something else. Sometimes our inner voice can get too loud and out of control. We figure we need to solve all our problems and heal all our pain immediately. Calm down; Rome wasn't built in a day, and if it had been, it wouldn't be nearly as charming. Go outside and run, walk, or go to the movies. Just don't stay in and play victim to your inner voice.

+ **Don't blame yourself.** What was wrong with the relationship is not wrong with you. Let's repeat: What was wrong with the relationship is not wrong with you. If the relationship was dysfunctional, that doesn't mean you are dysfunctional and are doomed to forever be in dysfunctional relationships. You deserve to have exactly the type of relationship you want. Remember, on some level, you chose this relationship. What was your lesson? How have you grown from it? Don't blame yourself by thinking you ruined everything. You were in this relationship to learn something that will help prepare you for your next relationship. Focus on learning rather than blaming.

+ **Forgive yourself.** Every relationship is a two-way street. Forgive yourself for the part you played. Be as loving as you can possibly be with yourself. Make your goal for the day to simply treat yourself with love. Every time a memory of the relationship surfaces, don't berate yourself for what you said or what you didn't say. Sit with the memory, feel the feelings, and forgive yourself.

+ **Be self-honoring.** Ask yourself every day if you are doing the most loving, self-honoring thing you can do for yourself at that moment. If you're not being self-honoring, then stop what you are doing. Part of being self-honoring is being completely and totally honest with yourself and those around you—even if it means that someone's feelings may be hurt.

+ **Take inventory of the good stuff.** You have abundance in your life. Sometimes, it may feel like you've got zipola. But you really do have a lot going for you. Take stock of the good stuff. If you can't see anything going for you, ask a friend to help you see it. Thank your angels, your Higher Power, and the people around you. When you realize what you have going for you, you break down illusions of scarcity.

+ **Stay present with yourself.** Delusional thoughts are often masks for the emotions you are feeling. When you recognize that your delusional thoughts are covering up emotions, breathe and allow yourself to feel your emotions in the present moment. These feelings are surfacing for your highest good. They are surfacing so you can heal. When you allow these feelings to surface and be felt, you are saying *yes* to your own empowerment. When you choose to stuff them back down, they never go away. Stuffed-down feelings come back to haunt you in your interactions with different people until you decide to allow yourself to feel them. (Ever find yourself having the same old problem with every new boyfriend?) Feeling can be very painful. They can also be cathartic and freeing. Often, people find very creative (and irrational) ways to avoid feeling.

Popular Delusional Thought: Let's Be Friends

The whole "let's be friends" thing is a myth. It's a delusion. It's said during a breakup to let everyone down easy. Don't be friends with your ex, at least not at first. In reality, staying friends immediately following a breakup can stall healing. Sure you can be friends down the road, when all the dust is settled and you are both glad you have moved on. But in the meantime, there are too many messy emotions, too many questions, and too much vulnerability. If you ever do become friends again, it's best to have a cooling off period first. After a time, if you see him around or in a group of mutual friends, don't get all huffy and confrontational—no noticeable lumps in your throat, no watery eyes, no "But why? Why did we breakup?"—Throw him into that group of acquaintances whom you don't call and don't spend much time with but who are pleasant to speak with when you do see them. After all, we can all use another friend.

It's okay to jump from lovers to friends only if:

+ One of you comes out of the closet. (Yippee! New gay friend!)

+ You weren't really in love with each other in the first place and your relationship went from platonic friends to unplatonic friends but never really made it to lover status.

Keep in mind that not every ex is worth keeping. Maybe you felt drained when you spent time with him, and he didn't support your goals. Why would you want to be friends? Becoming friends after dating is not necessarily the best evolution of a relationship. In fact, this breakup could be the easy way of getting out of a relationship with a bad friend.

The second option is far more tiring, less productive and complicated. Sometimes, we are in a rush to heal. We delude ourselves by thinking that if we go

POWER TOOL

Just Tao It

There are two ways to row a boat:

1. Row with the current, enjoy the ride and take what comes.

2. Row against the current, and focus solely on trying to get to shore.

Janice's Suppression Confession

I had moved to a new country to be with my boyfriend. I told everyone I had moved because of a career opportunity, but who was I kidding? I moved to be with him. I was lonely and scared, but determined to give this relationship my best effort. I wasn't happy but I deluded myself into thinking that everything was fine. I missed my family. The relationship with my boyfriend was rocky, and my new job was unfulfilling, but I put on a smile and pretended everything was okay. I refused to cry. After all, I was responsible for getting into that situation. All the while, I was suppressing many feelings.

After deluding myself into thinking everything was fine, I finally broke down. I couldn't hold in my feelings anymore. The floodgates opened, and I began to cry constantly. I felt immense anger, sadness, and fear that I knew I couldn't deal with alone. My feelings were surfacing so I could heal them. Luckily, Marni shared her successes with therapy and support groups. She gave me the courage to seek professional help. She even came to my first support group with me. Now, I think my Higher Power waited for Marni to enter my life so that I would have someone to turn to when I couldn't suppress my feelings anymore.

through an intense spurt of counseling and self-work, we can "get over it already." Then, we wonder why, after months, or even years, we find ourselves feeling emotions about our past relationships that we can't understand. When it comes to healing, row with the current. Stay present and take what comes. You'll get where you need to go when you are supposed to get there. The following are some fun activities to engage in when your thoughts are black and white:

+ **Have a revenge fantasy.** Sit back, close your eyes, and conjure evil scenarios about what could happen to him. (Insert evil laugh here. Mwah ha haaa.) If he obsessed about his hair during your relationship, imagine him waking up one morning to find he's bald. (Mwah ha haaa.) Or, if he was a workaholic, imagine him being fired. (Mwah ha haaa.) In real life, you don't wish these things to happen, but since you're in a state of delusion anyway, you might as well lean into it. It's healthy. (Mwah ha haaa.)

+ **Have a success fantasy.** After all, living well is the best revenge. Imagine that you're writing a book, and when he hears about it, he shakes with fear, thinking it's all about him. In turn, you get to say, "No Joe, contrary to what you think, it's not all about you." And then you walk away, leaving him with his jaw dropped, realizing how smart you are and regretting he ever stopped being with you.

+ **Go to a batting range and get out some rage on those balls.** Imagine each one is his head. It's being babyish, immature, catty . . . delicious. (Mwah ha haaa.)

Marni's Emotion Commotion

Feelings come up in me every day. Sometimes, I am not even aware of them. I just notice that I get tired and want to be alone. I don't want to talk to anyone I care about. I just want to be isolated and feel better. When I find myself in this state, my vices surface—I just want to watch TV or sit alone and eat to stuff things down and calm down.

However, at some point I'm aware of this desire to escape, and I take contrary action. (Not always, mind you.) I force myself to call a friend and be honest. I push myself to go to the gym. Or, I just notice my unhealthy desires and pick up a pen and write about what I really want: more love.

Whenever I feel as if there isn't enough for me, not enough space in this whole world for me, I can acknowledge what is really going on— feelings deep inside me are coming up to be healed. All I truly want is love and spiritual nourishment, not stagnation and excess food. After this realization, I can find in myself the courage to ask my Higher Power for more love.

Denial
Ain't Just
a River
in Egypt

enial can be terrific. Yay for denial! Denial serves a great purpose. It gets us through the worst of things. It's a survival tool that helps us cope with daily living while our heart aches from a breakup. Say you have an important presentation, but you just went through the wringer the night before when you and your schmucko boyfriend broke up. Denial helps you pretend that it never happened so you can get through the presentation with gusto and flair.

What We Resist Persists

With denial, we manage to float through the bad times until the day comes when we have a chance to work through the situation. Eventually, our psyche will decide when it is time to heal, and those feeling we were denying will start to creep up. We may start to feel tired and drained from spending so much energy resisting feeling what we haven't wanted to acknowledge during our denial phase. It is completely normal to push away things that are too challenging to cope with. We don't want to admit what really happened. But in the words of many comic book villains, "resistance is futile." The quicker you decide to embrace the truth of what happened, the better your whole life will feel.

Hidden Denial

Denial can be tricky. You can even go to therapy and hide in denial right there in the office. A lot of times denial can masquerade as you trying to figure out *why*. *Why* is not important right now. Figuring out why something happened will not make what has happened go away. We think that if we can only figure something out, then it will ease the pain. That thought is false, and it is rooted in a denial of reality. Yes, there is a time and a place to figure out why, but only long after we have thoroughly embraced what is.

Judgment Can Be Rooted in Denial

We judge ourselves for our feelings all the time. Try not to beat yourself up about feeling bad. It is okay to be miserable because you broke up.

Denying Can Be Fun

When it comes to relationships, we often blissfully deny the following:

+ The part we played in the termination of the relationship

+ Hidden resentments toward our ex

+ Past dating patterns and the fact that we replayed them with the latest ex-boyfriend

+ Not being completely over him. If it's only been a few days or weeks, prospects are doubtful that you're completely over him unless he was really awful. But if it's been a long time, you may be right. Trust your gut on this one.

How to Deal with Denial

The following are some ways to deal with denial:

+ **Ask a friend.** If you feel you're in denial, ask a friend to be honest with you about how she sees you dealing with the breakup. For example, Marni says, "Janice, I'm sad not to be with him because he was such a great guy and he made me feel so good. What do you think?" Janice replies, "You're forgetting that he wasn't all that great. He cheated on you. Someone who loves you wouldn't hurt you like that." Marni says, "I know, but he made me feel so good." Janice reiterates, "But he also made you feel so bad. Look at all the pain you're in. This is the same guy." Marni sighs, "But he was my best friend." Janice says, "But Marni, best friends are loyal. They don't cheat and lie right to your face." Marni sighs again, "I know but I just loved him so much. Why can't that be enough?" Janice replies, "That can be enough, if you're okay being with a guy who cheats and lies to you." Then Marni wells up.

+ **Admit it.** Marni says, "Maybe you're right. He was a jerk. My love for him wasn't enough. He cheated on me, and I wish it had never happened." Janice says, "It's good to see you admit it now." Marni wells up again.

+ **Sit with it.** At this point, Marni sits with the thought. She wells up, yet again. She gives herself a break. She stays home and drinks lots of water. She is nurturing herself through an overwhelming experience.

+ **Repeat.** There is always more to be uncovered. Recognizing our denial allows us to admit to all the feelings that we are having and thus, move on with our healing.

Realizing what we are in denial of makes us more vulnerable because we have to open ourselves up to the possibility of asking others for help. Friends are good at bringing us back into reality; you just have to ask.

Enter Gay Best Friend

Upon breaking up, you may be suffering from various forms of denial, most notably from the "but he was perfect" variety. It is at this point when you ask your gay best friend out for coffee to help you snap out of your denial. He'll remind you of what your relationship was really like. After all, he was there through the good times and bad. And, because he's a guy, he'll give you some insight into the male psyche.

If you haven't got a gay best friend, get one. Watch a few episodes of *Will & Grace* and you'll realize that every girl needs a male perspective of the homosexual kind. Plus, it's nice to have a true platonic male shoulder to cry on when the going gets tough. Other benefits of bringing in the gay best friend to see you though this denial period include:

+ He knows how men think.

+ He's honest with you.

+ He'll remind you of the times you called him up in a huff because of some issue you had with your boyfriend.

+ He's not like a straight guy who can potentially turn a meaningful conversation into a roll in the hay at your most vulnerable moment.

+ He'll make you feel gorgeous.

+ He'll adopt you during this period and take you out with all his gorgeous gay friends.

+ You can ogle cute guys together.

+ He's been through the whole coming out of the closet thing, so chances are he's been through denial, several forms of rejection, and bouts of feeling alone.

Realizing when we are in denial allows us to express our emotions rather than keep them locked up inside. Denial serves its initial purpose of allowing you to deal with feelings that are overwhelming, but when you are ready to move on (you will know when you are), allow yourself to be immersed in your feelings.

Don't deny yourself these activities:

+ **Go to a gay bar.** When you fall back into your denial and start thinking that the ex was more than he was, the gay guys all will pull you back and remind you that he wasn't so good in bed, that he wasn't so big, and that you were always left wanting for something more.

+ **Call a friend that you've been meaning to call for ages.** It's nice to catch up and get out of your head by talking about someone else's life instead of obsessing about your own. Also, if the subject of your past relationship comes up, you become a little more aware of what is going on inside your soul and how far you've come in your healing process.

+ **Watch a movie where the guy is a jerk.** This will remind you that it wasn't all rosy during your relationship. Some suggestions include:

  • *Sliding Doors* (starring Gwyneth Paltrow and hot Scottish guy John Hannah)

  • *Terms of Endearment* (starring Shirley MacLaine, Debra Winger, and Jeff Daniels)

  • *Bridget Jones's Diary* (starring Renée Zellweger, Colin Firth, and Hugh Grant)

Angerville

Once we regain our composure after the breakup, we might start to feel very angry. In other words, we head to Angerville. In this fiery place, he is always to blame. He is always a jerk. It is always his fault. It's okay to visit Angerville once in awhile. It can be very therapeutic to release those spiteful thoughts. That's the whole point of visiting—to deal with feelings and get them out of your system. Not many like to dwell in Angerville, however. So it's important to visit, get what you came for, and move on to the next town. Feeling anger is also a sign that you value yourself by not being okay with being treated badly.

The Main Drag

The main drag of Angerville can be fun and exciting. Being angry and fired up about him sure beats feeling guilty and worthless. Sometimes you get to the main drag, and you realize that you have spent so much time feeling "not enough" around him that you say "Wait a minute, that loser wasn't enough for me!" Be sure to allow your fire to blaze in a controlled healthy setting. Take a boxing class, play basketball, go dancing, get a carton of eggs and throw them at the wall in an alley. (Okay, maybe you should avoid illegal activities like vandalizing public property, but you know what we're getting at.) Scream, cry, and punch pillows. Create elaborate revenge fantasies. Revenge fantasies are a healthy part of the healing process as long as you don't act on them. Getting out frustrations is *so* satisfying. Don't ignore anger. It won't go away if you stuff it down. It will just manifest elsewhere in your life.

Blame Boulevard

On Blame Boulevard, we blame him for everything that went wrong in our relationship, which can be great fun. Or we blame ourselves because we enjoy the torture. Either way, we must pass through Blame Boulevard to get through town so here are a few travel tips.

On Blaming Yourself

First off, there is no sense in blaming yourself for everything. Blaming yourself is unproductive and a waste of energy. A relationship consists of two people, each equally responsible. Each puts into the relationship and each takes from the relationship. Give yourself a break. It's a relationship that you are only *half* responsible for. You're *entirely* responsible for your whole self, so concentrate on you instead of burdening yourself with all the problems that weren't even about you.

On Blaming Him

We often chide others for what we are not willing to see in ourselves. What is it that you find most appalling in him? Don't only name specific events or personality traits. Go deeper. What is underneath it all? What does it say about him? Do you display that negative quality in yourself? Whom do you treat that way? It's time to take some responsibility, girl. You are learning and growing with every step. Just the fact that you are looking at this book shows that you have an intention to work on yourself. So dig deep and take some responsibility for your process.

If He Is Blaming You

If he's blaming you, it's not about you. It's all about him. He is just upset. Don't take it personally. Breathe deeply and understand that his stuff belongs to him. All his baggage has his name on it, not yours. Hey, even the Dalai Lama gets moody sometimes; he just knows that it is about him and not about the world. If your ex tries to pick a fight with you, don't engage. You may be infuriated inside. Take a breath and smile. He wants to pawn his anger off on you. If you accept his baggage, it will weigh you down. You are in control of how you receive people. Remember, it's not your anger. It's his. And all you can control about his anger is your reaction to it.

Example: Blaming Him for Being Late

"I would hate it when he was late," could really mean, "I hated that he didn't respect my time. I wish he had been so enthusiastic that he could hardly wait to see me. I didn't feel loved when he was late."

Example: Blaming Him for Not Being Able to Read Your Mind

"I would hate it when he couldn't tell I wasn't in the mood to have sex," could really mean, "I hate that I couldn't express my feelings to him without being afraid of a negative reaction."

Angerville Isn't Actually Real

Angerville is a façade, like a movie set. Anger is really repressed sorrow and fear. The more you push away sorrow and fear, the more anger builds and builds until you have a full metropolis called Angerville. To avoid getting lost on the streets of Angerville, ask yourself: "What am I afraid of not getting now that I'm not in the relationship? Love? Satisfaction? Feeling special? I can still invoke these feelings on my own. They came from inside me;

they didn't come from him. So why am I truly sad? Is it the actual guy or am I mourning the death of the fantasy future I created in my head?"

Love may be a two-way street, but you only need to focus on cleaning up your side.

Angerville Practicality: He Still Has a Lot of Your Stuff

Spending time in Angerville can fire you up enough to give you the courage you need to tie up a few loose ends with the ex. For instance, along with emotional baggage, he may still have a few practical things you may want returned such as clothes, your hairdryer, jewelry, and so on. Now that you've broken up, you may be wondering how the heck you're going to get your stuff back. If seeing him again is a potentially danger-

ous situation, just forget about your things. Nothing is worth a black eye, broken arm, or verbal bashing. And all his things that you still have? Sell them on eBay.

If the worst that can happen is feeling weird and uncomfortable, call him up and set up a time to meet and get your things. This is a good time to return any of his things as well. Meet in a neutral location—neither his place (especially not his place!) nor your place. You may be scared, angry, or sad to face him, but you are respecting and standing up for yourself by stepping toward the closing of this relationship. Go girl! Be brave. Feel free to bring a good friend for support, too. When you see him, be civil and polite. You'll appear more powerful to him—even if you're not feeling powerful inside.

Patience (or lack thereof) in Angerville

"I want patience, and I want it now!" Patience while we're in Angerville is a precious commodity. We tend to get angry with anyone and everyone at the drop of a hat. So if you find yourself wanting to go postal while waiting in line at the grocery store, breathe deeply and remember that you are passing through Angerville. Though you may be blaming everyone in line for being slow, your anger isn't really about these innocent bystanders. It's a stage of your own healing. Instead of getting huffy at the slowpokes, imagine their stories and give them mental hugs. Before you know it, you'll be at the front of the line and serene in the moment. You will have gained power over your anger.

All in all, anger is healthy and normal. Even if your stay in Angerville feels uncomfortable, trust that it won't last long, providing that you express your anger in positive and productive ways. Soon you'll be on to the next phase of healing and you'll feel more peace.

Some Angerville activities include:

+ Practice an exercise you enjoy to burn off excess anger that's roaming around in your system. Take up martial arts, try swimming lessons, or just pump up the music and dance in sexy underwear.

+ Tenderize a slab of steak. Put the steak on a cutting board. Cover it with plastic wrap and smack it with a meat tenderizing hammer until it is as flat as a pancake.

+ Put on your sneakers, go for a run, and listen to angry music on your Walkman or MP3 player.

The Blue Period

A breakup just isn't a breakup without a bout of the blues. Depression can affect your whole body, not just your mood. It can affect your self-esteem, how you feel when you are with your friends, the way you eat, and the way you sleep. Basically, depression makes everything in your world feel harder. When you are depressed, it seems as if you have to drag yourself to do things that you used to do for fun. Everything seems boring and tedious.

Diagnosing Depression

The following are symptoms of depression:

+ Wanting to withdraw and hide from everyone
+ Loss of interest in things you once loved
+ Inability to experience pleasure and excitement
+ Fatigue and wanting to just lie around
+ Persistent boredom
+ Sleep disturbances (insomnia or excessive sleeping)
+ Uncontrollable crying
+ Change in appetite

+ Suicidal thoughts

+ Headaches

+ Excessive masturbation or no sex drive

+ Excessive exercise

+ Digestive problems

+ Restlessness, irritability, and anger

+ Feelings of worthlessness and inadequacy, as if you're not good enough

+ Time passing slowly

If you suspect that you are depressed, you probably are and that's okay. Join the party. Depression hits the best of us. In fact, it would be surprising if you weren't feeling depressed after a breakup. It is called a "breakup" because a part of your life that has been is now broken off. It is normal and perfectly acceptable to feel depressed and bummed out.

Recognizing Another Depressed Person

People who always seem angry or irritable, sad, or despairing may be easy to spot as depressed. But often depressed people are hard to spot because they appear happy-go-lucky and display little emotion at all. Many depressed people don't want to bring others down when they are depressed so they hide their emotions. Or they are in an environment where it's inappropriate to display their true emotions (for example, work). Often, depressed people also seek ways to cheer themselves up. That's why some of the greatest comedians have been known to suffer from depression. In fact, some of the happiest people you know could be either depressed, amply medicated, or both.

Depression vs. Sadness

There is a difference between depression and sadness. When you are sad, you feel like a sad version of yourself, and the feeling soon goes away. If you're depressed, your body, mind, and soul don't feel quite right. Depression colors your whole life. And the feeling doesn't soon pass as it does when you're sad. The good news is that depression is usually self-limiting, meaning that it will eventually improve. Unless you suffer from clinical depression, these feelings will pass. You're not alone, however, if your depression persists and you think you are suffering from clinical depression. Over 10 million Americans do.

The factors that influence depression include:

+ Heredity

+ Tension or stress

+ A traumatic event

+ A chemical imbalance in the brain

+ Constantly being around a depressed person

+ A poor diet and exercise regime

How to Break through Depression

Depression is as much an illness as high blood pressure. You can't just get over it as you can sadness. Nor can you just get over it by putting a smile on your face. Depression is a real illness that is not going to vanish if you ignore it.

Physical Healing

Heal your body to heal your mind. It may sound strange that taking care of yourself physically can help you mentally. In fact, achieving physical health is possibly the most important step you can take in healing depression. First off, you can actually increase the severity of depression if you don't give your body the nutrients and care it requires. Your body gets cranky, and this crankiness can lead to more severe depression. Second, when we experience a traumatic event such as a breakup, we have a tendency to forget about our health regime. We can binge or not eat altogether, not sleep or sleep too much, not exercise or overexercise, or turn to excessive drinking and drug use. After a breakup is no time to skimp on your health. Push yourself to stay in your daily routine. Do the footwork even if you really (really) don't want to. Remember, by physically taking care of yourself, you're healing your mental self.

Fatigue Fighters

One of the most common symptoms of depression is fatigue. That's because your body, mind, and soul are working to heal you from this breakup. Healing takes energy. Here are a few ways to avoid fatigue and boost your energy:

+ **Eat well and often.** Mini-meals maintain your blood sugar level. Low blood sugar can lead to bouts of depression. Making healthy food choices fills your soul with strength and energy.

+ **Water yourself.** Thirst makes you sluggish. Dehydration also lowers blood volume, making your heart work harder. You are probably dehydrated right now—go have a glass of water.

+ **Move.** Regular exercise keeps your mojo up. It releases seretonin and other happy brain chemicals.

+ **Sleep.** Your body does its restorative work and processing while you sleep. Give your body time to absorb the physical, mental, and spiritual work you do all day. When you sleep, cuts heal, pimples diminish, and your mind rests. Give your body a break and get yourself to bed. Conversely, don't

POWER TOOL

Can't Sleep? Here's a Smelly Solution.

Lavender is known for its relaxing and sleep-inducing properties. If you can't sleep, pour 5 or 6 drops of lavender essential oil on a cotton ball and set it on your bedside table to smell as you doze off to sleep.

oversleep and throw off your regular sleeping pattern. Maintain a regular sleep schedule to keep your internal rhythm in tune.

Food and Mood

Be your own nutritional detective. Find out if part of your depression is related to your diet. Here are some signals your body sends to tell you that food may be affecting your mood.

+ **Low energy/fatigue.** You may be skimping on carbohydrates, your body's primary source of fuel. Also, you may not be getting enough iron or water.

+ **Feeling down.** Go fish. You may not be getting enough omega-3 fats from actual fish, or enough B vitamins and folic acid. Eat more fish, beans, bananas, and whole grains.

+ **PMS.** Got milk? Consuming less milk and more sugar can exacerbate PMS, which is not such a good feeling. Cut back on the sweets, and reach for more calcium and nuts.

+ **Constant hunger.** Chances are you're not eating enough, or not eating enough of the right foods. When life feels out of control, restricting food sometimes seems like a good way to seek control, but it is not. Spread your meals evenly throughout the day, and eat balanced meals. Not treating your body right will not give you more control in your life.

+ **Binging and craving.** It's easy to forget all about the balanced diet after a breakup. This can lead to skipping meals and binging, which leads to the cycle of skipping more meals and binging again. Eat balanced small meals throughout the day, and you'll be less likely to binge. Beware of refined sugar. It gives you fast energy, but it can also make you feel as if you are pasted to the sidewalk. Get a natural energy boost from fruit and water. Not only will you avoid the sugar blues, but your energy will also last longer.

+ **Shakiness and anxiety.** It's possible you're relying on caffeine or cigarettes to give your body a boost or simply not eating enough food, rather than eating enough of the right foods to give you energy throughout the day. If your body is not being fed, you need to eat. Eat more carbs, and choose decaf.

+ **Mental fogginess.** Not eating enough antioxidants and skipping meals can make concentration difficult. Eat more veggies and nuts.

POWER TOOL
Thank Your Heart

Your heart works hard to keep you alive—even when it feels broken after a breakup. Thank this pumping miracle for all the work it does on your behalf, and ask it what you can do to help it do its job. Does it want more exercise? Sleep? Healthier food? Listen to and fulfill its request. Thanking your heart helps you to feel more centered and enjoy the present moment.

Mental Healing

The roller coaster of emotions you feel after a breakup is actually a good thing. Feeling your emotions means you are healing. It means that you are not bypassing them or suppressing them, but going through them. It's a normal part of the process of healing. Pushing these feelings away or stuffing them down will never make the situation better. Let them stay with you until they are ready to pass. By doing so, you are healing.

Confusing Emotions

Sometimes, you may feel sad and not know why because:

+ You were damn glad to be rid of the guy.

+ You are already with someone new and wonderful.

+ You just plain don't understand how you, such a together individual, could be feeling sad and empty over a silly boy.

Be with these feelings anyway, even if you don't understand why you have them. Let them pass through you. Take your time feeling them. Write about them, paint them, dance, sing . . . whatever works to give your feelings voice and expression. Some of the best bodies of work were created after big events such as a breakup. Maybe your breakup will help you tap into a well of creativity. Your body and mind are naturally working through the healing process.

Repression = Depression

One thing is certain: Distractions aid us in covering up our feelings . . . which is also known as repression. Repression leads to depression. Just for today, sit with whatever you are feeling. Notice what you are feeling when you want to distract yourself. Let that feeling be okay with you. It will soon pass. If you repress feelings that come up, they will hide out in your body. Think of the word "repression." To repress. To press down.

Freud said repression is a "mechanism by which individuals protect themselves from threatening thoughts by blocking them out of the conscious mind." Sure, repression serves a purpose as a survival tool in the beginning, when what is coming up is too overwhelming to handle. But, long-term repression can lead to stress, which is the main cause of all kinds of health issues (not to mention bad skin, bad hair, and overeating). We are actually far stronger and capable of taking in more than we ever thought possible.

Resistance Is Irresistible

Most of us go to great lengths to avoid our feelings. This is normal. Resistance is something we all experience. You are not alone. Feelings don't have to feel good, but they do have to eventually be felt because they will never go away until they are expressed, accepted, and forgiven. Studies show that feeling your feelings is the best way out of them. It has been proven that if you want to feel better, you have to let yourself feel worse first. You will always get what you give, no more, no less. If you try to escape your feelings by not feeling them, later in the day you still won't feel that fantastic. However, if you really let yourself feel the worst, when you come out on the other side your experience of joy will be that much deeper.

> *"People that feel their feelings impress me far more than those who always seem to have everything under control."*
>
> —*M. Kamins*

Nobody Has Ever Died from an Uncomfortable Feeling

If you feel sad, allow yourself to feel sad. Rent a sad movie, and cry the whole day with tea and tissues. If you feel rage, don't try to calm down. Feel it. Just don't punch anyone in the face. Paint an angry red painting with your fingers or play violent video games. Let yourself get through your feelings. They will pass once you feel them.

> *"I once called a friend and said 'I'm so lonesome, I don't know what to do.' She said: 'Just be lonesome, it will pass.' And it did."*
>
> —*M. Kamins*

What doesn't kill you will save you.

Professional Help

A feeling of dread may arise upon the suggestion of professional help. Luckily, we have arrived at a moment in time when seeking professional help for problems is not only accepted but encouraged. Having a good therapist working for you can be the most effective tool in healing. That, and reading this book.

The Stigma of Therapy

There are a million reasons why people don't want to go to therapy. A big reason is that people think that only people with *real* issues go to therapy. People who are really screwed up, spoiled, selfish, rich, crazy, unintelligent, and holier-than-thou go to therapy. Normal people do not go to therapy. People who are just kind of sad do not go to therapy. Besides, what do you talk about with a therapist?

The Truth about Therapy

Going to therapy is not a sign that you have one foot in the nut house. Instead, you are daring to take control of your life, understand yourself better, and figure out how to have a more fulfilling existence.

A therapist is an objective observer whose sole purpose is to assist you in growing. Therapists help you become aware of your tendencies and help keep the focus on you so

Janice's Fear of Therapy

I thought I was able to handle my breakup alone, thank you very much. But I was beginning to scare myself when I started constantly crying uncontrollably; I knew I needed help. I called the EAP hotline (Employee Assistance Program, a free counseling service available as a benefit in some corporations), and they hooked me up with a therapist.

I didn't know what I would say when I got to the therapist's office. Did I tell the therapist that I'm sad about my boyfriend and breaking up? What? Like a thirteen-year-old girl? I felt silly for not being able to control my emotions. I felt stupid for making an appointment in the first place. But mostly I was fearful that I would walk into her office and start crying. I walked into her office and within two minutes I was crying. I cried the whole session. I couldn't stop. I talked through my tears. The next visit, I cried more. Same thing on the next visit. I started bringing paper towels to the sessions because they were more absorbent than tissues.

She didn't judge me for crying. She listened. She gave me advice. She told me all about depression and chemical disorders. She sent me to a psychiatrist who prescribed some antidepressants. She seemed to know exactly what I needed when I needed it. I am so glad I could go to someone who could take care of me and help me see through the fog.

I still cry a ton, and I still don't fully understand why I cry like I do, but I now know that crying is healthy not stupid. I'm learning so much about myself that I would have never learned had I not started going to therapy.

that you don't get sidetracked into thinking of everyone else. Sometimes, people have a therapy session every day while they are coping with a crisis. Others have one session a week. People go to therapy for as little as a month or as long as twenty years. You can go for as long as you feel that therapy is helping you.

Therapy helps you learn about yourself and your relationships. We are all only knowledgeable about the warped version of our own relationships. Therapists are knowledgeable about hundreds, maybe thousands of people who experience the same feelings as you do. So, you really get the expertise of thousands of people in one convenient fifty-minute session. It's really a bargain. You get a fuller life. Priceless.

Even My Dog Is on Prozac

A popular and effective treatment for depression is antidepressant medication. Antidepressants help if you have a chemical imbalance whereby your body doesn't release "happy" chemicals (such as seretonin) effectively. A psychiatrist prescribes antidepressants, technically called tricyclics, seretonin reuptake inhibitors, monoaminine oxidase inhibitors, and lithium. Different drugs take different amounts of time to kick in. It could take a few days or several weeks for the drugs to be fully integrated into your system. Often, these drugs must be taken for six months or longer to stop depressive symptoms.

There are also natural remedies that are said to boost those "happy" chemicals in your brain. St. John's Wort and folic acid are two examples.

Reach for Support

Reaching out to people for help is very important when you're going through the craziness of a breakup. When you reach out, you'll find you're not as crazy as you may have thought. Support groups are completely free and nonjudgmental. You won't lose a thing by going to a meeting and checking it out. Quite the opposite. You can gain a whole new outlook on life.

At support groups, people share what is going on in their lives. When you listen to their stories, you may hear many of your own. And you can choose to share your stories or not. People in support groups don't judge. They have been where you are. They understand and are available to listen.

Popular official support groups include:

+ Overeaters Anonymous: *www.overeatersanonymous.org*

+ Sex Addicts Anonymous: *www.sexaa.org*

+ Alcoholics Anonymous: *www.alcoholics-anonymous.org*

POWER TOOL
Don't Sit in Your Own Crap Just Because It's Warm

Don't get too comfortable sitting at home with the curtains drawn. Put on a cowboy hat, slap on some sunscreen, and head out to experience the world. If you put in the effort and go out into the world, your Higher Power will grant you wonderful things.

- + Adult Children of Alcoholics: *www.adultchildren.org*
- + Al Anon/Alateen (For families of Alcoholics): *www.al-anon.alateen.org*
- + Debtors Anonymous: *www.debtorsanonymous.org*
- + Narcotics Anonymous: *www.na.org*

Unofficial support groups include:

- + Dogs and cats
- + Books
- + People in houses of worship
- + Hobbies
- + The person who serves you coffee every day

Friends You Can Fart With

Breaking wind can break the ice. Do you have people you feel comfortable farting around? If you do, go hang out with them. If you don't, it's time to eat some beans and evolve a relationship or two. You don't have to be blatant and rude about it, but be comfortable enough to fart and fess up. You want to be able to say "Excuse me, I farted. Don't come over here. It smells." Flatulence is the sign of true friendship.

Creative Vortex Friends

Be around people who inspire you! These are people who get your creative juices flowing. They are interested in what you are pursuing. They encourage you and remind you of your own wonderful talents. Show your stuff to them. Accept their compliments without apology. We thrive with encouragement. Don't be afraid to seek it. Don't be afraid to get yourself out there and share your talents. Never apologize for being who you are and pursuing what you love. Together, you can channel a creative vortex just by being creative in the same space.

POWER TOOL
Bake Bread

Bread is the symbol of family and friendship. Bake and break bread with those you are grateful for. Not the culinary type? You can find a quick "just add water" bread mix at the grocery store or use the recipe for Friendship Pretzels on page 75.

Unsupport Groups

Unsupport groups are those that don't support your greater healing, don't watch your back, and encourage your self-sabotaging behavior.

Break up with Friends Who Aren't Supportive. Breaking up with friends is harder than breaking up with lovers. It's hard to say you don't want to be friends with someone anymore just because you don't like being with that person. However, if you have a friend that you are happier not to be around, then stop hanging out with him or her. This is where you need

Friendship Pretzels

RECICE

1 tablespoon yeast
1/2 cup warm water
2 or 3 tablespoons honey
1 teaspoon salt
1 1/3 cups all purpose flour

Optional ingredients: Sunflower seeds, golden raisins, cranberries, chocolate chips, sesame seeds, or whatever sweet surprises you would like your friends to find in their pretzels.

Dissolve the yeast in the water. Add honey and salt to the yeast mixture, then add the flour and knead for the dough for a couple minutes. Roll out strands of dough and make fun (phallic) shapes. Brush the pretzels with a beaten egg so they look nice and shiny. Sprinkle with salt and sesame seeds. Bake 10 minutes at 425 degrees.

to be your own best friend and stay away from people who aren't supportive. Tell them you need to nurture yourself through this difficult time and you want to be left alone. They'll probably be more understanding now than if you told them out of the blue that you want them to take a hike.

Beware of Vampire Friends. Vampire friends, like real vampires, are not always easy to spot. You can't always sense them while you're with them, but you can always sense them afterward because you feel drained and tired. What do vampires of legend do? They drain their prey of its life force. They suck your blood to make themselves more powerful. Vampires don't kill you because they know that you will generate more blood to replenish your own blood supply, and thus they can feed off you for years if you let them. In the grips of a vampire, you will go on living, but you will constantly feel drained, tired, and suppressed. Sometimes vampire friends will drain you within a two-minutes phone call. Other times it takes months of feeling tired and drained to finally realize that the most loving thing for you to do for yourself is stay away from that friend.

Beware of Antiregularity Friends. Stress, dehydration, and crappy eating can all lead to your being plugged up. Or, if you're around people you don't feel comfortable with, your plumbing could come to a screeching halt. If that's the case, it is a sign that your body is holding in and is not relaxed. It is a sign that you need to spend some time on yourself. Drink some water and go for a walk. Are there any emotions your body is holding in? Relax and say the affirmation: "I easily release that which does not serve me." Then grab some literature and spend some quality time in the loo.

Beware of Mojo Squashers. Mojo squashers are those who don't support your dreams wholeheartedly. They are fond of dishing out advice in the form of "you should . . . " Sometimes, they think it is their job to tell you if your dream is worthy. At times, you may even find yourself agreeing with their the bad advice! They are dream-draining mojo squashers. Get them out of your life immediately. The mojo squashers in your life can also be your relatives. It's not so easy to get rid of them. Instead, make them aware of their mojo squashing habits in a kind way. You could be teaching them a valuable lesson and helping them on their own journey, plus your honesty about their behavior could get them off your back.

Poetry for the Blue Period

Through the works of others you can figure out what is going on deep inside yourself. Poets write about their truth so that we can relate to them. Their poetry can facilitate epiphanies.

+ **Read thought-provoking poetry.** Powerful words from the mouths of women can make you feel less alone because they can convey in words what you are feeling. Some of our favorite poetesses include Anne Sexton, Mary Oliver, and Nikki Giovanni.

+ **Listen to spoken-word poetry.** Two emotional and inspiring poets available on CD are David Whyte and Saul Williams. Ohhh, very passionate.

+ **Write your own poem.** After some inspiration from the masters, write your own poem. It doesn't have to be Pulitzer Prize winning. It doesn't have to rhyme. Just write what you feel. Sometimes, it takes a couple pages before anything true comes out. Be honest. No one else has to read what you wrote.

Today, class, we are going to talk about what we learned from dating all those boys. Each boyfriend teaches us something we need to know about ourselves. And if we haven't learned our lessons, we are to forever repeat them with future boyfriends until we do. We call this the curse of the unlearned lesson.

Men are sold "as is." You can't change a man so don't try. It's not your job. Make it a rule never to sign up for changing anyone but yourself. Learning lessons from each relationship helps you improve yourself. We can't blame them for what went wrong, we're the ones who agreed to go out with them in the first place. Evaluate the part you played in your relationship. When you break up, take what you've learned from the relationship and vow not to do the same thing again . . . lest you be cursed with the unlearned lesson.

So how do you learn this lesson once and for all?

Step 1: Awareness. Recognize the faults you saw in him. That may seem easy if it was a bad breakup. But remember that people who do heartless things are in pain. Recognize that he might have been scared or lonely or felt inadequate. Step into his shoes to see the person behind those traits. You may recognize some similar traits of your own. We are all attracted to someone who is like us in some way. Remember that everyone hurts sometimes. Everyone wants love. Everyone struggles to find his or her own way. Your ex-boyfriend (hopefully) wasn't trying to be an evil person. Find compassion for his faults and the emotions he was feeling during the relationship.

Step 2: Acceptance. Accept that you have faults, too. You wouldn't recognize his faults if you didn't have them yourself. Just as you wouldn't recognize jealousy in other people if you didn't know what the concept of jealousy meant. Mother Theresa felt nothing but compassion for the killers and rapists she visited on death row because all she knew how to feel toward herself was compassion. She had no self-hatred and could therefore not see hatred in others. These are not faults; they are just places where you still have work to do. Recognizing and owning these traits is huge.

Step 3: Action. Take action by learning how to improve and strengthen your soul through these faults. To do this, walk through your memories of the relationship. Sit with the feelings that arise. Listen to your heart. Let

POWER TOOL

Call a meeting with your multiple personalities

+ *The career girl*
+ *The girl afraid to be alone in a crowd*
+ *The girl who is happiest swinging on swings*
+ *The sex fiend*
+ *The movie star*

Call a conference with all the roles you play, and decide which personalities should stay and which should go. Say goodbye to the ones that no longer serve you.

yourself feel the feelings and don't berate yourself for feeling them. If you listen to your heart, give yourself time, and are nurturing to yourself, you'll learn from your relationship and become a stronger person. You'll become the person you are meant to be. And, you'll find the person you are meant to be with. Maybe the whole reason for your breakup was to prepare you for the lucky man of the future. And maybe, while you're preparing to be with him, he may unknowingly be preparing to be with you.

Get Real about Your Faults

Honesty is the best policy. It's best to be honest with yourself first. Are you a faker? Whom are you trying to kid? Whom are you trying to please? If you can't be honest with yourself, how will you find honesty in others?

The following are activities to break the curse of the unlearned lesson:

+ **Go to a new section of the bookstore.** Humans are creatures of habit. Part of going into a new section of the bookstore is to break your old habits. The old cliché is true: if you always do what you've always done, you'll always get what you've always got. Look in the Photography section; go to the Self-Help section; flip through books in the Antiques section. Open yourself to something new.

+ **Add a new activity to your exercise regime.** If you've always wanted to take horseback riding lessons, make a plan to do it. If you always go to the gym, go ice-skating instead. Join an intramural team. Not only will you use new muscles and release tension, but you may also find something new that you become passionate about.

+ **Go to an ethnic grocery store.** Pick up a recipe book, buy different ingredients, and then get cooking. If you're not the culinary master you wish you were, invite a friend to help you through the recipes.

+ **Woo yourself like the man you've always wanted to date.** If you want him to be the type of person to play you songs on the guitar, take guitar lessons. If you want him to be a hiker, go hiking. In doing these things, you may just find the lucky guy of the future and break the curse of the unlearned lesson.

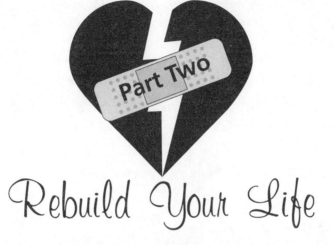

Rebuild Your Life

Now that you're not in courting mode and gallivanting around town with Mr. Man, you may have noticed that you have buckets of time, energy, and space in your life. You may feel excited, nervous, happy, ecstatic, empowered, and curious about what you are going to do with your newfound freedom. Or you may see this as a void in your life, which makes you feel lonely, sad, scared, stressed, angry, and uncomfortable. All these feelings are totally understandable and acceptable, and are being felt by a gazillion people all over the world. Your challenge is to love yourself through these feelings.

You are on the precipice of a new phase of life. Where do you go from here? Now is the perfect time to do things that improve you and propel you into alignment with the person you truly are. There is a girl inside that hasn't seen the light of day for a while. Let her come out and play. Reevaluate your deepest desires, reconnect with yourself, and build on the most important love affair you'll ever have—the love affair with yourself.

Build Your Own House

Here's the thing. Your intimate relationship can be like a big house that's made up of your bricks and his bricks. When you break up, he takes all his bricks away, and you take your bricks away. The bricks head in separate directions. If you weren't ready for this or didn't expect it, it could feel like an earthquake just destroyed all you loved. That could be a big shock. That could be embarrassing, like someone unexpectedly coming over when your house is a mess.

Did You Lean on Your Man?

Most women feel uncomfortable acknowledging that they may have leaned on their man to define who they are. We all lean sometimes because we need support. Leaning is okay as long as it does not cause us to feel less independent or badly about ourselves. Leaning means that you love yourself enough to ask for what you need. The goal is to love yourself. While you are in a relationship, it can sometimes feel as if the goal is to love your man as best you can so that he will be happy, and thus you will be happy. However, the true goal is to love yourself in good times and bad, no matter what.

What Does "Being Loving to Myself" Look Like?

Being loving to yourself means taking good care of yourself. It means eating well, getting enough sleep, brushing and flossing your teeth, getting haircuts and pedicures, giving yourself time to decompress after a long day. . . . Basically it's about allowing yourself the pleasures of life. By doing this, you are building a strong foundation of who you are, of how you expect to be treated, and of what you won't put up with from anyone. If you treat yourself well, you'll expect others to treat you the same. You'll attract men who will treat you as well as you treat yourself. Water always seeks its own level.

Rebuilding Your Home

It would be nice if our houses were made up of only our own bricks—built and ready to live in before we get into a relationship. However, then we wouldn't get to learn all the lessons we are meant to learn from our relationships. In a sense, having the foundation of our house challenged will make us more stable in the end, as long as we don't give up.

Picking Up the Pieces

After a breakup, we pick up the fallen bricks and rebuild. In essence, we are forced to date ourselves, to build our homes on our own ground, ground that we can love and tend and know down to the last square inch. At first our home may not seem as cozy without him.

But we can also trust that though we appreciate the help of a strong and hefty man, we don't need him. We will feel more empowered on our own.

Filling in the Gaps

It may be tempting to look to excessive eating, alcohol, drugs, or a new man for extra support and to fill in some of the gaps in our house. However, filling the gaps with these vices will just make us feel used up and tired. These vices are the opposite of being loving to ourselves. When you feel the need to turn to these vices, your soul is really signaling that it has extra energy that needs to be used up. Lucky you. Use that energy to love yourself. We need to be aware of self-destructive tendencies and remember to use our own bricks for strength, not waste.

If we do choose to fill the gaps with these sorts of distractions, we must be aware that we are looking to escape and not be fully present with ourselves. We are giving ourselves amnesia from our feelings, and those feelings will eventually come back. Ask yourself how the distraction is working for you. Is it loving and nurturing? When our feelings return (and they will return), if we then choose to hide again, we can become swept up into a vicious cycle.

Constantly ask yourself: *"What is the most loving thing I can do for myself in this situation?"*

"The biggest human temptation is . . . to settle for too little."

—*Thomas Merton*

The following are activities to help you build your own house:

+ **Make a collage.** Clip pictures from magazines that provoke something in you. Sometimes after clipping a few pictures, you'll come to realize that your collage has a theme. The theme might be about how you want your new life to be, or it might be about where you're at emotionally. Allow the theme to reveal itself to you.

+ **Redecorate your space.** You are in a new phase of life, so update your surroundings to match. Add a few knickknacks, remove a few pictures, move stuff around, and give stuff to charity. Go to thrift stores, garage sales, and flea markets. They can give you great ideas on changing the look of your space.

+ **Revamp your address book.** Some acquaintances may not fit into your new life. People who drain you or don't support your dreams are not worth having in your new life. (See Chapter 6, "The Blue Period" for more details.) Cut off the dead weight. Erase or cross out their names. Or, buy a new address book and only put in people who made the cut into your new life. Doing this feels like making a strong decision to support yourself.

9

Date
Yourself

Were you waiting until you were engaged to get a new set of dishes? Decided not to paint your bedroom walls because you figured you'd soon be moving in with him? We can do silly things when we put "us" before "me." And now, after the breakup, the future is wide open. Vow that from this day forward, you will live for you in today. You will paint your room fuchsia if the mood strikes you. You will buy the pink flowery dishes you've had your eye on. You will plan and live every moment *just for you.*

Make a Play Date with Yourself

Push yourself to go places alone, even if it feels lonesome and scary. In doing so, you are energetically reaching out to the world. Get dressed and go before you chicken out. It may feel scary, but act as if it feels empowering. Soon, you'll convince yourself that it isn't so scary. At

first, go to places where being alone is the norm. Head out to coffee shops, the local botanical garden, the beach, museums, bookstores, and matinees. Bring a journal or a book for company. Write letters. Hell, write a whole book. That's what we did. If you're really adventurous, take yourself on a long drive and explore a new town for the day. Do what really excites you. Do what you really want. Appreciate that you don't have to wait for anyone or compromise your plans. Write down what you really want. Writing it down helps you define it. Then, make plans and don't flake out on yourself. Put more of yourself into the world. The more comfortable you feel spending time alone, the less alone you will feel.

POWER TOOL
Soup Time

Spend a whole afternoon consciously not multitasking. Just be. Spend the afternoon making homemade soup with vegetables you picked up from the farmer's market. Revel in cutting vege-tables, smelling the broth, and adding spices. Spend high-quality time with yourself. Remember, it's your life and your time belongs to you.

Take Yourself out to Dinner

Going to a restaurant alone for the first time is a wonderful, scary, and brave experience. At first, you may feel uncomfortable and think you're the biggest loser on the planet. But ask yourself "What's the worst that can happen?" Make believe that you love your solitude; get excited about having so much time to yourself. If you act as if you are excited to be on your own, your old pattern will change so that you will actually start to relish your alone time. If you are very nervous about what other people think while you're taking yourself out for dinner, assure yourself that what they think is not of importance. To do this, put your hand on your belly and assure the little girl inside that you are taking care of her and she can trust you.

In taking yourself out for dinner, you are creating a new space for adventure to occur. For the first outing, bring a book or your journal if you want company. You'll increasingly feel more comfortable every time you take yourself to dinner. One day, when someone says, "What?! You go out for dinner alone?" you'll say, "Yes, of course. Don't you?"

During dinner, touch yourself gently on the knee under the table. Hike your skirt up a little if you're feeling frisky. Over lobster, discuss where to take yourself on vacation. Make plans for the future. And remember to send yourself thank you flowers the next day.

Create an
Empire

With all this free time on your hands, you can start investing in Me, Inc. The time after a breakup is a chance for personal reflection, a chance to reevaluate your goals and rediscover your heart's deepest desires.

Do It Now

I'll do this when I have more money, when I'm feeling prettier, thinner.... Don't wait until you've reached a certain level of satisfaction to do what you want in life. *Today is the day!* Act as if you are doing right now what you were meant to do. What would that be like? Acting as if will create a fire in your belly that will glow for all to see.

Pursue Your Dreams

Put your dreams on paper. Be specific. Go for it. The universe will reward you when you follow your dreams. By putting your dreams second to the gamut of things you have to do every day, you get swept up in priorities that are of no importance in the long run. When you don't pursue your dreams, at least a little bit at a time, you are actually postponing happiness by wasting energy on activities that are not truly important.

Fear Factor

Do what you fear the most. What is the worst that can happen? You fail? You will also learn. Sometimes the lesson teaches us more than the achievement.

Do It Badly

Deep down inside you know what you want to do. What are you waiting for? Afraid you can't do it? Do it anyway. Do it boldly. Do it badly. At least you're doing it. The difference between you and the person who did a bad movie last year is that she went out and did it. The very action of starting and doing something shows your intentions to the universe, and you will be rewarded for your efforts.

The following are activities for creating an empire:

+ **Make a dream list.** Write down twenty-five things you want to accomplish. Then, decide what you want to achieve in the next year, in the next three years, the next five

POWER TOOL

Interview Your Heart

Tune into your heart by asking it a few questions:

+ *What is your secret wish?*
+ *What is your favorite thing to do?*
+ *Who makes you leap?*
+ *What drains you?*
+ *What pumps you up?*
+ *How do you wish to replenish your energy?*
+ *What do you want right now?*

years, and so on. Look at your list for this year. Break it down further into baby steps. Completing even a small goal gives you a place to focus your energy and gives you a sense of success and self-improvement. A big goal is only a bunch of little goals all put together.

+ **Act as if you've already achieved you goal.** If it's a financial goal, write yourself out a check for the amount you're going to earn. Or, when you walk around town, walk with the knowledge that you already are what you want to be.

+ **Dream big and allow fate to help the dream come true.** Go crazy. Let anything be possible. Your life can be as big as you want it to be. Dreaming about it is a prayer to your Higher Power who will help make your dreams come true by putting signs in your path. Be open to seeing the signs.

The
Void

As your authors know only too well, having a new void in your life can easily be filled with certain vices that tend not to serve your highest good. All these vices are just distractions. Trust us, they do not help. They only make you feel more empty. You will never be glad that you chose to distract yourself rather than feel. Feeling your feelings can be both exhausting and utterly satisfying. At the end of the day, we have never said, "Gee, I am so glad that I ate junk food all day instead of feeling my feelings, going about my day, and eating well." Studies have shown that when people feel sad, angry, tired, or lonely—feelings often associated with a breakup—they tend to want to medicate these feelings with whatever works to make them go away as fast as possible. We tend to unconsciously create unhealthy habits because somewhere in our warped mental state it seems easier to engage in self-destructive behavior than to focus on what is going on in our lives.

Common Distractions to Fill the Void

Common distractions to fill the void include overly focusing on food or body image, chemical intoxication, or even just making sure you are so busy all day that you don't give yourself one minute to sit down and breathe. Distractions are different for different people—basically whatever works best to take the edge off. Not all distractions are negative either, once in a while they are okay, even beneficial. However, it's not healthy when these distractions become a way of life or an everyday coping mechanism.

Stuffing It Down

Don't get us wrong. Eating can be fabulous and passionate. Food can be sensual and orgasmic (and organic). Eating should be pleasurable. That said, eat consciously. Unconscious eating to fill the void can be harmful, confusing, and disempowering. It may feel good, great, even empowering in the present moment, but take our well-seasoned advice. In the long run—*it sucks to stuff*. Stuffing is not—at all—part of your divine purpose on this earth.

If You Can't Stop Binging on Food

Look in the phone book under Overeaters Anonymous (OA), and call your local chapter. Or find them online at *www.overeateranonymous.org*. Find out when the next meeting is, slam the refrigerator door shut, and get to the meeting as fast as humanly possible—even if you feel you have to stop and binge on the way. Tell them you need help. Overeaters Anonymous is free, and the only requirement for joining is "a desire to stop eating compulsively." Let yourself reach out. There are other people who have been in your situation. You are not alone. Receive the help others want to give.

Marni's Stuffed up Feelings

I avoided feelings for most of my life. I still find myself seeking distractions from my feelings. When I was in college, I would either eat junk food all day or make the entire focus of my day about what junk food I was going to eat later. When I broke up with the most serious boyfriend I ever had (the person I thought that I would marry), I found that I didn't really feel sad. Instead, I was very busy. I had no job, but I was the busiest unemployed person I had ever met. When I found myself at home alone with nothing to do, I would look through the refrigerator and snack. I never wanted to be alone with myself. I felt like I was going to die if I had to sit alone with myself. Finally, I realized that I was terribly sad and hurt. I felt like something was seriously wrong with me. I hated feeling that way. It was lonely and it sucked. So I let myself mope and embraced my feelings. Guess what? After a while, they passed. It was so satisfying to move through my feelings. I still battle myself, but I am getting better.

Think of what it is that your heart desires, your greatest goal in life. Know that *more food will never bring you closer to that dream*. Never ever. Your greatest dream might be to feel inner peace. You can't reach inner peace through food.

Creative Vortex

If you don't know what to do with the feelings you wanted to stuff away, channel that energy into a creative vortex instead. We overeat to stuff down fear and anxiety or to push away love and intimacy. Sometimes, we overeat because we are feeling so much (good things or not good things!) that it seems as if we can't contain ourselves. We repress our feelings. (Don't forget, repression leads to zits and depression—more of what you don't need.) At other times, we are not ready to hear that we really are amazing beings. (F.Y.I.: We are.) Eating doesn't help because not only are the feelings still there, but now we're gaining weight, too. Channel those feelings into a creative vortex by writing a poem, story, or journal entry.

Fear Inventory

If panic or fear has set in, rather than stuff your feelings away make a fear inventory to let that fear out. Write a list of everything you're afraid of at that very moment. Don't prefix it with "I am afraid that . . ." because in doing so, you are reaffirming fear. Very counterproductive. Just start writing. When you define your fears by writing them down, you learn how to overcome them. You release fears from your body. Then read your list. See what you can change and accept what is out of your control.

Marni's Fear Inventory at This Moment:

+ I may never have enough money.
+ My stomach is getting bigger.
+ Wrinkles
+ My metabolism is slowing.
+ My boobs are saggers.
+ Soon Mr. Man might get sick and tired of me and not think I'm attractive anymore.
+ Doing a scene in acting class.
+ Doing a monologue in front of people.
+ Looking like a frump.
+ My mom will get mad at me.

Marni's Gratitude List at This Moment:

+ Janice
+ Clean pillow cases
+ Flirting with cute boys
+ Magazines
+ The ocean
+ My family
+ Books and bookstores
+ A movie in bed with popcorn and a friend
+ Soft blankets
+ Mani-pedi's
+ Flavored lip balm
+ I am feeling love
+ I get to go to sleep tonight in a warm bed
+ Tea in big mugs
+ Vanilla soy milk
+ My brain

Review Your List

Notice that most of your fears are not actually occurring at that moment, so you can let them go. You can always revisit them later, but for now you can get through the moment without so much fear and anxiety. By writing down your fears, you make yourself aware of them and they are no longer hidden inside. Fears love to hide out in your body. Don't let them. Snuff them out and be rid of them. Try a fear inventory and see what happens. To be rid of today's fears, ask your Higher Power to remove these fears. Then rip up your fear inventory and throw it away. You are no longer controlled by your fears.

Gratitude List

The very next thing you do after a fear inventory, even if you don't feel like it, is to make a gratitude list.

God Boxes

God boxes are great. You don't have to believe in God to have one; you just have to believe that somewhere in the world there exists a power greater than yourself. This power could be a power such as the ocean, electricity, the mountains, the moon, anything that adds a spiritual feeling to your life. It's a power that is greater than you and has a power to make things happen that you can't. Decorate a box and write your innermost fears and desires on pieces of paper and put them in the box. It's like sending God a letter. Put your fear inventory in the box, too. When you put your fear inventory in the God box, you are asking for your Higher Power to remove those fears. You're letting go of them and giving them up to the universe. God Box building instructions:

1. Find a cigar box, stationery box, or any darn box you fancy.

2. Decorate the box (optional).

3. Write your deepest desires, worries, fears, and dreams on pieces of paper.

4. Put them in the box to give them out to the universe.

Do the footwork and leave the rest to God.

Other Uses for the God Box

You can also use a God box to hold mementos of the relationship that you aren't ready to get rid of just yet. Love letters, photos, movie tickets, and so on can all spend some purgatory time in the God box.

+ **Photos.** Review the photos of the two of you as a happy couple. Notice how cute you are and how not cute he is. Do some of those smiley photos remind you of other angry, frustrated, or empty emotions you were feeling even though you appear happy on the outside? Observe that moment. Notice that it wasn't all flowers and candy. Don't forget the negative stuff. It's through the negative stuff (as well as the positive stuff) that we grow.

+ **Love letters.** Give yourself time to reread them. Make it a moment. Schedule a date with yourself to do it. Read the beautiful things he wrote, the silly words, and, possibly, the broken promises. Then, throw them all in the box.

+ **Movie tickets, theater programs, and other mementos.** If keeping a memory of an event will provide some intrinsic value and remind you happily of the event, then keep the memento. If the memories remind you more of the person you were with and less of the event itself, toss the memento. (Consider eBay if it's something someone else will value. You could heal and make some dough all at the same time.)

What Is Your Heart Hungry For?

What is it that you really want in life? What does your heart crave? Here are a few ways to feed your heart something other than food:

+ Bathe with yummy smelling bath salts and bubbles.

+ Soak in a whirlpool (if you've got one, or grab a friend and sneak into a fancy hotel like little whirlpool bandits).

+ Rent a movie and get under the covers.

+ Make tea and drink it outside wearing sunglasses.

+ Take a nap.

+ Wash your face and put on a facial mask.

+ Go to a CD store and listen to new music.

+ Dance as if no one's watching.

+ Go to a cool office supply store to marvel at the potential of newborn paper.

+ Call people that understand about "stuffing" and reach out for support.

+ Lie on the couch and let your feelings be felt.

+ Frantically write a poem (pen to paper, no stopping).

+ Paint.

+ Draw.

+ Read something fun and inspirational.

+ Be of service to someone.

+ Go for a walk.

+ Get a mani*cure*, pedi*cure*, or both.

+ Go to yoga.

Get messy and dirty and paint all night. Read for hours. Rent movies you've always wanted to see, and host your own movie marathon. Dance to sexy music wearing nothing but a feather boa. Let yourself sing! Take a class you didn't make time for before. Make a turkey dinner with your friends—even if it's not Thanksgiving. Revisit a hobby you once loved. Get passionate! Fill up your buckets of time and energy with activities you love.

Definitely do things that scare you.

Get Lost

Head out the door with no destination in mind. Just believe that you'll figure out where you're going when you get there. Who knows? You could meet a soul mate. Or, you could solidify the story line of the screenplay you've been thinking of writing. Let your mind wander. Listen to nature. Listen to people around you. Listen to yourself. When you aren't concerned with where you are going, your mind is free to wander.

Create a Ritual

Add a new ritual to your daily life—a small thing you do just for you, not something for your boss, your mother, or your ex. Go to the Farmer's Market every Wednesday. Make soup on Sundays. Get your nails done every other Friday. It should be something that makes you happy.

Passionate Activities

Here are some passionate activities to help you learn what you love:

+ Listen to a favorite CD while fingerpainting naked.
+ Make a scrapbook.
+ Go to the beach—listen to the waves on the rocks.
+ Host a slumber party.
+ Belly dance.
+ Read in the children's section at the bookstore.
+ Go to coffee houses to listen to local artists sing.
+ Attend books signings.
+ Cruise yard sales for tchotchkes.

+ Get touchy-feely with your beautiful body.
+ *Hola!* Learn to speak Spanish.
+ Write a letter to your mom and send it.
+ Dance naked.
+ Visit cats and dogs at shelters.
+ Collect inspiring quotes.
+ Memorize your favorite poem.
+ Go on vacation alone.
+ Celebrate singlehood with a *Sex and the City* marathon (you can rent the entire series).
+ Take a pottery class, and give friends your homemade signature mugs.
+ Hike down a trail you've never been on before.
+ Take a day trip with a group of friends.
+ Bake cookies for your friends.
+ Sing songs loudly, passionately, and sexily.
+ Take a photography class.
+ Go horseback riding.

Learn
What
You Love

109

+ Read poetry in the tub.

+ Host a tea party—make everyone wear a hat.

Warning

If you don't use your energy for fun and expressive endeavors, pent up energy will fester in your body in the form of stress and may wreak all kinds of havoc. Stress hormones affect every cell in your body. When you've got a lot of stress in your body, your immune system shuts down. You may experience:

+ A headache

+ Bad hair

+ Stress zits

+ Sore temples

+ A sniffly cold

+ A skin rash

+ A pain in the neck

+ Sore shoulders

+ A fat ass

+ Insomnia

+ An itchy head

+ Cellulite

+ Joint pain

+ Cold sores

+ An aura of bad energy that no one wants to be around

+ A tummy ache

+ Severe flatulence

Reclaim Your Space

There may be certain places you avoid because you're afraid to see him there. Or, maybe you don't want to remember the times you went there happily together. Reclaiming your space is all about confronting the fear of visiting places you avoid because of him. The more you go to the places you don't want to revisit, the easier it will be to stop allowing the breakup to have power over you. You will instinctively know when you are ready to reclaim certain spaces.

Take Power Away from Your Fear

Each time you choose to confront fears, you empower yourself, and the universe rewards you. When you allow fear to surface, you are allowing it to be healed. If you are afraid that you might see him somewhere, know that if your Higher Power wants you to see him, you'll see him and you'll know what to do in that moment. If you aren't meant to see him, then you won't.

Worst Case Scenario:
You See Him and He's Got a New Fiancée

While you're bravely reclaiming a bookstore you both once

loved, you see Mr. Commitment Phobic, and you discover he is now betrothed to another. Although the news may be painful, the real rub is that he beat you to it. Your fantasy of running into him while you were strutting down the street with a big fat diamond on your finger and a much hotter boyfriend on your arm will now never come to pass. Remember:

+ It's not that she is better than you, it is that she is a better fit for him. Just like, somewhere out there is a man who is a better fit for you.

+ His fiancée will have to deal with his annoying habits. You will not.

+ Rejection is God's protection.

+ It is darn fantastic that you are no longer with his self-centered self.

Our Higher Power sometimes does for us what we cannot do for ourselves: Maybe you would have taken years to realize that he was not the one for you. Now that he's officially off the market, you know for sure that you were not meant to be with him.

Reclaim His Side of the Bed

Why are you still sleeping on "your" side of the bed? Whom are you saving all that extra space for? A half-empty bed can be one lonesome place for the recently single. After all, you may have spent a considerable amount of the good times right there between the sheets. Now, along with the obvious lack of shagging, there is the absence of spooning, tickling, laughing, late-night talking, and early morning gazes into each other's eyes. You could be avoiding "his" side of the bed because it still holds remnant male aura. Replace this aura with more of your own so you can reclaim the queen you had before he came along. All this new space can be very luxurious. Spread out, pass gas wherever you please, and feel the splendor of sheets that don't smell like raunchy hairy boy.

How to Reclaim His Side of the Bed

1. Scoot your bodacious body to the middle of the bed.
2. Don't look back.
3. Scoot further so you are decidedly occupying the space he once claimed as his own.
4. Make snow angels.

You won't be able to resist smiling.

Reclaim Bad Spots

Reclaim the places that remind you of why you are relieved to not be dating him. Maybe it's the IHOP down the street where you fought all the time. If you revisit old places and create new memories, the old memories will fade faster. Sure, you may reason that you would never ever step one impeccably pedicured toenail into that IHOP again for many reasons—bitter coffee, runny eggs, bad service. But ask yourself this: Are you looking for other negative excuses not go back because you're afraid?

Go in. Order your eggs. Sip your coffee. A wonderful event will occur. You will know a new peace. Maybe the eggs are still runny. Maybe the coffee is still bitter. But the vibe of the joint has shifted. Enjoy the peace. Second cup, please.

Reclaim Good Spots

Afraid to revisit that charming B&B where he first told you he loved you? Afraid it will be too much to bear? Reclaiming the good spots you went to together can be tougher than reclaiming the bad spots. In the bad spots, you can experience new peace. In the good spots, you're just reminded of how happy you were and how different it feels without him. Revisiting the good spots keeps you from closing yourself off to wonderful parts of the world. Avoid them and you're only punishing yourself. *It's all about closure.* Revisiting the good stuff also helps you feel your emotions and release them all. Get out any toxic feelings that no longer serve you.

Bonus: This is a great opportunity to connect with friends. Reach out, plan a girly weekend to a B&B, and head out to the IHOP. Kick up your heels and have fun healing!

Connect With Your Higher Power

Everyone has Higher Power. Some people refer to their Higher Power as God, the Force, Spirit, Allah, Jesus, an angel, the Universe, the Ultimate Being, Tarot, a fairy, an ancestor, a guardian angel, and so on. Your Higher Power is a power greater than yourself and it can be called any name and take on many forms. Throughout this book, we refer to "It" in different ways. It's a part of every religion, yet no religion. When we refer to the Higher Power or God, we don't connect this being to a specific religious entity. Wherever you believe your Higher Power originated from (whether it be religious or otherwise) isn't as important as the fact that your Higher Power exists and loves you.

Where?

People seek a connection with their Higher Power in church, synagogue, the forest, and even in the ocean. Some people light candles and pray. Others meditate. Some connect in the shower. There is no one correct way to connect to your Higher Power. The importance lies not in *how* you connect, but in the fact that you *make a connection*. Just having the desire to connect is enough. Connecting to that power is what feeds our soul and fills us up with light. It also keeps us from feeling alone. When we are connected, be it once a day or once a year, we feel safe.

What?

You might have a random thought that seems to come out of nowhere, such as, "I should call my friend Samantha and see how she is." Then, when you call she says, "That is so funny. I was just thinking about you." That is your Higher Power telling you something. You might even get a gut feeling that you can't explain, such as, "don't turn down that street." Your Higher Power is talking to you and working around the clock to ensure that you are on the path you were meant to be on. You just set the intention to talk to God and *listen* to God.

Love and forgive yourself for any judgments you have placed on your relationship with your Higher Power.

Serendipity

Serendipity is the faculty for making fortunate discoveries by accident. Your Higher Power is constantly putting events and thoughts in your path so that you can make fortunate discoveries by "accident." When you feel uncertain about the outcome of an event, or when you just want some company, look for signs from your Higher Power. Let them be your guide.

You're exactly where you're supposed to be.

Reopen the Connection

If it's been awhile since you chatted with your Higher Power, here's how to reopen the connection.

Select Your Environment

Your environment may be a beautiful and special place. You could hike up to a vista at the top of a mountain with the intention to connect with your Higher Power. You could sit on the grass or on a rock or in a tree. Your environment doesn't necessarily have to be some place beautiful. And you don't have to make a pilgrimage to a church, synagogue, or other place of worship. It can be in your car, before you walk into a party, at work, in the bathroom, or at the kitchen counter. You can also create instant ambiance anywhere by lighting a few candles.

"One of my favorite places to talk to God is in a ladies room at work. There's something so gratifying about locking the stall door, taking a few moments to breathe and say hi to God."

—J. MacLeod

Open a Dialogue

Simply say something like "Hello. It's been a while since we chatted. Bygones. I'd like to know you again. This is what is going on in my life." You can also close your eyes and think about an issue you want guidance with. If you don't have a specific question or facet of your life to focus on (work, love life, family, a certain person), you can ask your Higher Power to simply guide you toward the life you are meant to have. Just start talking and start listening—even if your belief doesn't feel strong. Take an active interest in the changes in your life. Our Higher Power answers through the events, people, and nature that surround us. You can also try these writing exercises to help open the connection:

+ **Write your Higher Power a letter.** Write your Higher Power a letter and ask to feel a connection. Be honest about your feelings and desires. Then, give your Higher Power a chance to respond. Write whatever thoughts come into your head. Those thoughts are your Higher Power talking. Take dictation.

+ **Write a want ad for a guardian angel.** Don't think that you have a guardian angel? Have you ever asked for one? To get a guardian angel, write a want ad, as you would requesting a friend or lover. Ask for the qualities you want. Be specific and honest. Angels will listen and fulfill your request.

These chats and writing exercises are actually prayers. Prayers don't have to be about seeking redemption, forgiveness, or other damnation-type notions. Prayers are open conversations with your Higher Power.

There Are a Million Ways to Pray

You can sing, dance, chant, draw, or write to your Higher Power. Add prayer to the activities you love. Find prayers in the language that works for you. Not only will you enjoy the activities more, you'll receive messages that your Higher Power wants you to ponder in the present moment. If you're not comfortable just winging it when praying, no problem. Here's a nondenominational prayer you can use to start opening the connection.

> **Serenity Prayer**
> *God, grant me the serenity to accept the things I cannot change,*
> *The courage to change the things I can,*
> *And the wisdom to know the difference.*
>
> —*Anonymous*

Pray Often

The more you pray, the more comfortable it becomes and the easier it becomes to recognize and read messages from your Higher Power.

Expect a Miracle

This isn't as tall an order as you may think. Miracles happen every day. Your Higher Power has an overview of everything that is happening on earth. Something you do that seems small can lead to a miracle for another person. And vice versa. Your Higher Power may use something that appears negative, such as a breakup, to bring greater joy into your life later. After all, you can't find Mr. Right when you're still dating Mr. Wrong. And you can't necessarily be in a healthy relationship when Mr. Right comes along if you haven't learned lessons from dating Mr. Wrong.

Your Higher Power Answers

No heartfelt prayer ever goes unanswered. Prayers are always answered in one of three ways:

+ Yes, here you go.
+ No, not yet.
+ Wait, I have something better.

Maintain the Connection

Communication in a relationship works two ways—one talks and the other listens; then the other talks while the first one listens. You can't just pray and expect to hear the answer when you're not listening for it. The light is in you and all around you. All you have to do is call it forth and listen.

Take Your Higher Power Out for a Drive

Drive to a destination. Get out of the car. Open the passenger door for your Higher Power. You are surrounded by a powerful entity, a creative force, an energy from something greater than yourself. When you are consciously aware of this force around you, you invite serendipitous events to occur. Don't stay home. Explore the world with your Higher Power as your travel companion. Amazing things will happen.

Feng Shui Your Space

Feng shui is the art of opening up energy flow in your home. By rearranging your furniture according to feng shui principles, you increase energy flow and invite serenity into your space.

POWER TOOL

Let Go

Let go and move with changes as they come into your life.

Connect with Crystals

Crystals hold energy. Some crystals are so strong that they vibrate in the palm of your hand. Visit a crystal shop and pick up one crystal at a time. Find one that feels just right. Put it on a chain to wear around your neck or stick it in your bra. Use it as a reminder of your connection with the universe and your angels.

Celebrate the Season

Sometimes, we get so distracted that we fail to notice nature changing all around us. Look up at the sky. Look at the ground. Look at the trees, and feel the air around you. Surrender yourself to the season. Let yourself change with it.

Listen for Songs

"I can't get this song out of my head!" Listen to the songs that play in your head. They carry messages. These songs can bring you insights into your emotional state and guide you on your path. Just as a movie score aids the plot, the songs in your head let you know what's going on with you emotionally.

Go to the Beach

Synchronize your breathing with the ebb and flow of the waves. Water is a strong and powerful force. It's God-like. Ocean waves move to a rhythm that no human being can control. Sometimes, we try to change the things we can't control. This is futile. Let them go.

Take a Hike

Connect with nature and listen to the trees. They are talking all the time. Hear what they have to say. They release positive energy and willingly absorb energy you wish to release as you walk among them. They also like hugs. It might feel silly to hug a tree, but it will make you smile. Try it.

POWER TOOL

Everything Happens for
a Reason

*Sometimes God does for us
what we cannot do for ourselves.*

Look Up

Feeling blue? Check out the sky—blue, gray, cloudy, clear, bright. The sky is always beautiful, even on stormy days. Its God-like immensity can add perspective to your day. Right now you are exactly where you are supposed to be.

Message from God

Hello. This is God. I will
be taking care of all your
problems today. I will not
be needing your help. Relax.
I've got it covered.

Part Three

Back in the Saddle

You will intuitively know when you are ready to start dating again. Let yourself ease into the saddle. If you're not ready to get back in the saddle, listen to yourself, and give yourself time. Trust that your Higher Power will bring you the right person at the right time. In the meantime, cherish your solitude. If a man appears, he doesn't have to be the next *one*. He could just be someone you enjoy spending time with for now. It's okay to date casually if you want to, but never settle for a lover that you don't truly enjoy being with. Remember, you're inviting this person to share in your life. He is lucky to be in your life. Don't let just anyone in. When you do that you are coming from a place of scarcity. There are always enough fish in the sea.

Worst Case Scenario: All My Eggs Will Dry Up Before I Find the Man of My Dreams

First, you're delusional. Second, children will come when the time is right. Your Higher Power has a plan for you, and it is better than your wildest dreams. Life in the saddle will be a lot easier if you just let yourself trust that you are where you are supposed to be and let your body be in sync with the horse. Worrying about what could happen in the future does not serve us *at all* in the present moment; it only makes us fearful and shaky. Animals can smell fear. We often have outrageous thoughts. If what we are worrying about isn't actually happening, then we are being delusional.

When Are You Ready?

What if you never want to date again? If the thought of dating again makes you want to hurl, then you are not ready. Period. Don't force yourself into it. There is nothing wrong with not being ready. If you're dating someone new and you're scared to be physical, then don't be physical because you're not ready. Any man who can't wait for you to be ready is absolutely not worth it. Drop that cowboy. Being scared is a gut reaction. Listen to your gut. Take it slow.

You Are Not Ready for Another Relationship if:

+ You're absolutely terrified to put yourself out there because you fear rejection.

+ You're still checking messages daily hoping that your ex will call.

+ You keep looking for your ex everywhere you go.

+ You don't make plans with friends just in case your ex asks you out.

+ You don't feel as if you have had ample wallowing time.

+ You go out on a date but feel as if you're cheating on your ex.

+ You're not excited about cute boys. In fact, you don't even notice them.

You Are Ready for Another Relationship When You:

+ Begin to notice other boys in a positive way.

+ Stop looking for your ex in places you both used to visit.

+ Stop reading your ex's horoscope.

+ Get butterflies in your stomach when you meet a new guy.

+ See a cute guy in the elevator and fantasize that he will grab you and push you against the wall and kiss you passionately.

Your Ex Is Ready for Another Relationship When:

+ He never calls you. When you call him, he's distant and sounds bored.

+ You notice a big change; for example, he used to always call and now he only e-mails.

+ He rarely replies to your e-mails and voicemails. He's trying to send you a *silent sign*. People often use silent signs when they don't know how to face a potential conflict. He doesn't know how to communicate his feelings. He still really wants you to think he's a nice guy, and he feels guilty about wanting to move on. Though it sucks that you can't read his mind, you also can't teach him how to communicate. It's not your job. Just accept his silent sign.

He's Got Another Girl* When:

+ He tells you.
+ He used to take you out for brunch even when you weren't dating anymore, but suddenly he is never available. He's taking the new girl out for brunch.
+ Now when he spends time with you, it's early in the week. Your status has been downgraded. He reserves the weekends to be with her. (P.S. Why are you still hanging out with your ex-boyfriend?)
+ He says he's going out with friends on Valentine's Day. He's got a date.
+ Suddenly "work," "friends," or "band rehearsal" are all places where he has to stay late.
+ He has no interest in hearing about you or telling you about himself.
+ On second thought, who cares if he has another girlfriend? Be glad you're not her.

*If he's dating someone else, it does not necessarily mean that he is completely over you. It may mean that he's thinking with his penis. Blame nature. That's all you can do.

The following activities will help you know if you're ready to get back in the saddle:

+ **Go to a local trendy coffee shop.** Watch the guys come in. Notice the ones that you think are cute. Find one that you are particularly smitten with. Do you want him to be your boyfriend, or even your date? If you find yourself saying, "Yuck, I don't want anyone, no matter how cute, to be my boyfriend," then you have your answer. If you find yourself intrigued or curious about his life, you may be ready to entertain the thought of dating again.

+ **Ask yourself if you have taken down the pictures of the old cowboy.** If you haven't, then you probably aren't over your ex yet.

+ **This may be a little x-rated, but . . . .** Whom do you think about when you masturbate? Your ex? Generic man with penis? Or the hot guy from the coffee shop?

{"image_type":"page sidebar text","content":"The\nBREAKUP\nREPAIR KIT"}

{"image_type":"page number box","content":"130"}

The Old Cowboy Rides Back into Town

It wouldn't be surprising if you and your ex wanted each other back. Getting back together is like putting on an old pair of jeans that you trust will always fit you the same way—and it's not as scary as trying on a brand new pair. So when he comes swaggering back into your life and makes you weak in the knees, what do you do?

Don't get back together too soon. We'd hate to burst your bubble, but don't forget the reasons you broke up in the first place. If you're thinking that he's really sincere about getting back together, ask him what will be different now. If he can't answer, tell him to come back when he has an answer. In the meantime, spend time dating your fabulous self . . . and others.

Honesty is the best policy. Don't convince yourself you want him back because you feel guilt or a sense of obligation. You have to want him back because you honestly believe with all your heart that you could picture yourself living happily with this person again.

Revamp the crap. In order to not repeat history, you both have to define the reasons you broke up. You both have to decide you want to change how you are together. Remember, the definition of insanity is doing the same thing over and over again and expecting different results. If you both are not 100 percent recommitted, shake hands and say so long.

Don't just start over where you left off. Let this be a new beginning. Make him woo you. If you're not excited about being with him, then don't be with him. It sounds simple, but sometimes we choose not to believe what we really feel. We sometimes believe that the best scenario after a breakup is to get back together. But then, if we do rekindle the romance, it feels wrong. If you feel drained and crappy after getting back together, then your gut is telling you to get out. Be brave. Trust your gut and stick to your guns. Say no to what you don't truly want. You will energetically be opening yourself up to something much better.

The Booty Call

Don't accept his booty call invitation. If he comes running back within the week, stay cautious. He could be making a booty call and could just be craving some intimate attention. Sadly, men have been known to think with their penises. Even if he dumped you, he and his libido are forced to break the habit of getting a piece of your hotness. No one can change his tune within a week. If he comes crawling back, asks for booty and gets it, you could be setting yourself up for postorgasm disappointment. Don't listen to his preorgasm thinking. Don't listen to your own either. It's warped. If you don't think you'll be able to resist the temptation, don't shave your legs, wear bad underwear, and masturbate before you see him. Do whatever you have to do to ensure that you can say no and stave off your own cravings.

Signs of His Preorgasm Thinking

Signs of his preorgasm thinking incude:

+ He's late. (He's not respecting your time.)

+ He doesn't care about what you want. (He's not respecting your needs.)

+ He wants to have sex with you even if you're not interested. (He's not respecting your body.)

+ He doesn't offer to walk you to your front door at the end of the night. (He's not being a gentleman.)

The Old
Cowboy
Rides
Back into
Town

133

In bed, most men will go as far as you let them. It's your job to call the shots.

Signs of Your Preorgasm Thinking

Admit it. There are a few warped thoughts that go through the head of a girl who is considering a roll in the hay with Mr. Ex, such as the following:

+ "It's not like my magic number will go up." (The number of different guys you've slept with.)

+ "I'm mostly looking to scratch an itch." Use your fingers.

+ "I can have meaningless sex with him." No such thing.

+ "It feels good and I like sex, damn it." Again, use your fingers, or go to a sex shop and get yourself some fun toys.

POWER TOOL
Visualization Before Jumping in the Sack

When tempted to jump in the sack with your ex, do some visualization exercises. Imagine lying next to him in bed after you've slept with him. Are you:

    a. Happy
    b. Confused
    c. Angry
    d. Disgusted
    e. Dying to bolt out the door
    f. Lonely

Chances are, if you chose a. Happy, you will be wondering where you stand and will therefore become confused, then angry, disgusted, want to bolt, and feel alone. Correct Answer: g. All of the above.

+ "No one will know." Why would you want to have sex with someone that you are embarrassed to talk about having had sex with? Get some balls (yours, not his); stand up for yourself. You will feel more self-respect.

+ "Maybe we will get back together." If this is the case, get back together first, *then* have sex, and in the meantime rent some porn.

With all that said, sometimes when we think we are craving sex what we are really craving is that deep connection to another human being. It's that innate fear of being alone. What you need is some good wholesome fun, and fun isn't something you need your ex-boyfriend for. Call up your girlfriends for a spa day, sink into a bed with a juicy novel, or go to a video arcade with a roll of quarters.

A Word About the "M" Word

If you're unfathomably horny for your ex and don't think you can stave off your preorgasm cravings, then give yourself an arm hickey. Just kidding. Honestly, this is the perfect time to masturbate, masturbate, masturbate. If you've never gotten yourself off, it's about time you started. It's a wonderful release. And, it will keep you from having breakup sex with him, which can get really messy and complicated.

Boys begin the wonderful act of masturbation early in adolescence. For girls, it often takes a little longer. There is a crazy social stigma connected to girls who masturbate. If you feel shame, get over it. There is no reason guys can wack off shame-free, while girls walk through life with pent up energy and shame. To masturbate, relax and start touching down there. If it feels foreign, go buy some erotic literature to get you in the mood. (Scared to buy porn? Ask your gay best friend to take you to a good sex-toy shop, and you can buy it together.) Explore yourself and discover what makes you feel good. Or, buy yourself a vibrator. If you're too embarrassed to go into a sex shop, there are Web sites devoted to helping women get comfortable with pleasuring their own bodies. (A handheld "massager" from the drug store will also do the job.)

> *"The gorgeous lady teacher . . . makes me play with myself in front of her and she teaches me all the different ways to give myself pleasure. . . . She tells me to always know how to give myself pleasure so I'll never need to rely on a man."*
> —*Eve Ensler,* The Vagina Monologues

How Do You Deal With His Cheatin' Heart?

So you broke up because he cheated on you. That slime. Now, you're thinking of getting back together but you are cautious. You may subscribe to the "once a cheater, always a cheater" philosophy, which makes it difficult to take him back. Before you think of getting back together, evaluate whether his indiscretion had something to do with what was happening in your relationship. Why did he stray? Are underlying issues at play? Consider evaluating what really happened (besides the obvious indiscretion).

Evaluate the situation. Your relationship may still be salvageable, depending on the extent of the cheating. (Example: He's been cheating on you for years as opposed to he got drunk one night and had an indiscretion. Both violated your trust so neither is okay, but the latter is more forgivable.) If he has been cheating on you for a long time, you need to let him go. Not because it means that you no longer love him or he no longer loves you. He may love you a lot, and you may think that he is your soul mate. However, you need to love and respect yourself enough to know that you won't stay with a man that has been cheating on you. It is about self-respect.

Actions speak louder than words. If it is about a drunk night of indiscretion—again, all you know for sure is that actions speak louder than words. His actions showed that he does not take your relationship seriously. If he says he does take this relationship seriously, wait and see what his actions say. If he lied right to your face, he is the perfect candidate for repeat cheating. Lose the liar. He is so not worth it. If he felt terrible and guilty for what he did and confessed right away, the two of you could work this out.

What's the cheating really about? He did it for a reason that he could not speak up about. Maybe he feels unhappy or trapped. Maybe the cheating was a symptom of a bigger problem in your relationship. Maybe he just needs to grow up. Are you both willing to work through the problems? Are you sure you want to give up your time to wait and see if he will change? If you immediately think that he is not willing to work on the underlying issues of this indiscretion, then he doesn't deserve you back in his life. He has to be willing to work on himself, just as you have to be willing to work on yourself. Both of you have to remain humble and teachable.

It wasn't about you and it wasn't your fault. Above everything else, know that when men cheat, it's not about you. It's about them. They're being too weak. Too weak to tell you something wasn't working for them. Too weak to control themselves. Not man enough to do the right thing even if it's hard. Do not use his indiscretion as an opportunity to beat yourself up by thinking that if you were prettier, thinner, or better in bed this wouldn't have happened. There is nothing you could have done to prevent this. He needs to grow up and get some integrity. You need to keep your own.

It must be over between him and the other woman. Don't even bother getting back together if he is deciding whom to choose—you or her. You owe it to yourself to get out immediately. Never be second fiddle. And as for knowing if he's telling the truth about it being over, trust your gut, and don't let yourself ignore obvious signs just because you want him back badly.

Get the goods. Get all the gory details out in the open so there are no surprises later. You'll know your bond is strong if he can tell you about it and you can listen. This exercise will force him to be really honest, and it will force you to really digest the truth of what happened. Leaving it up to your imagination is dangerous. Ask questions. It's not easy, but if you want it to work, you're relationship may need this spring cleaning.

Work together. He has to be just as keen as you are in working through this problem. Talk, talk, talk. Listen, listen, listen. Communication is key.

Start over. Both of you can't really pick up from where you left off. The cheating is already out there and can't be undone. Start from the beginning, and make him woo you. Make him reearn your affection. If he's not willing, he's not worth it.

Forgive and forget. These are not just words. You really have to forgive him and you really have to forget the mistake he made. You're bound to have moments when your mind races, and you conjure worst case scenarios. When this happens, stop, take a breath and think before you act. Madly tracking him down, falsely accusing him, or otherwise acting paranoid will do no one any good. If you're not prepared to recognize this, then you are not prepared to reconcile with him. Hear him out, then have him hear you out. Forgiving and forgetting means never bringing up the situation again. Ever. And the truth is, you may be able to forgive, but you may never truly forget.

> **POWER TOOL**
> *Brunch*
>
> *Brunch is a very romantic meal, even after a night of fighting. It's one of the universal times to make up and laugh again. It is almost as good as after-fight sex. It is a wonderful "talk about the relationship" date. The sun is shining, there is a smell of freshly-brewed coffee in the air, and there is a full day of possibility ahead.*

Perform a romantic rekindling activity. You could make it official by holding a little candle-burning ceremony to extinguish the old flame and rekindle your own. It may seem corny, but it will be fun and show that both of you are willing participants. Plus, it's a nice prelude to makeup sex.

When
Do You
Stop
Loving
Him?

Kow do you know you aren't in love with him anymore? This is a toughy. This is where you have to trust your instinct. Knowing when you are not in love anymore is different for everyone.

Janice's Account: Listening to My Reactions

This is where I had to trust my instincts. I simply asked myself if I still loved him. Early on, my first reaction was a definite yes. Yes, I love him. Eventually, the answer was yes, but it hurts to love him. Then, it was yes because I feel I should. Was I wrong all this time? It felt so right at first. At some point, I asked myself if I loved him, and the answer was no. I smiled. I felt a weight lift off my shoulders. I was finally free from my self-inflicted obligation to love him. Sure, I care for him and I wish him well. But now my heart is free.

Marni's Account: Lesson of Love

I think that for me, it was more about trying to get him to truly love me. To see what I could do to make him love me, and how much I could get away with and have him still love me. I don't know if I ever felt the love that I was constantly trying to feel about myself through him. However, when he was good to me, I felt that must have been love. So I loved him back because I felt like he must have been such a good person to love me. But after a long time, even after breaking up, I realized that I had always felt drained and unsupported by him. I felt like he wanted to consume me rather than let me fly. That didn't feel like love anymore, it made me feel sad and empty. I realize that I will always care about him. I still wonder what he is doing and what he is working on in his life and if he is happy. I really want him to be happy. However, I was not happy inside when I was with him, and that is how I know that even though I love him, I am not *in* love with him.

Rebound Relationships

If you're thinking you should run out and boink every boy in the 'hood to make yourself feel better, or at least make you feel as if you're over the ex, it won't work. It's just another way to avoid the pain and temporarily feel wanted. If you opt for a few rolls in the hay anyway to cleanse the palate, be sure you are safe and are the one calling all the shots. Don't do anything just to please a guy who wants you. Remember, guys who will want you are a dime a dozen.

The rebound boy is very tempting. He's like a shiny new car. Eye candy. No dings or rust spots, and he looks like he'll be a smooth ride. Anything would be better than that old jalopy boyfriend you had before. The rebound boy eases the pain of a past love, but could also be a way of covering up unfelt emotions from your last lemon lover. Generally, rebound relationships are doomed from the get-go. If you think this new guy isn't a rebound, then *take it slow*. If you end up breaking up, start reading this book over.

> *"Boys are like new cars. They're all shiny at first, but eventually the shine wears off and the rust shows through."*
>
> —*Aggie MacLeod (Janice's mom)*

If You Are in the Midst of a Rebound Right Now...

A rebound relationship is not necessarily a bad thing. Rebounds can be fun. Sometimes the best way we can end one relationship is by starting another. It gives us closure. The reason that rebound relationships are so common is that they are a perfectly normal form of healing. Just try not to put too much importance on this relationship if it is indeed a rebound. Rebound relationships rarely work out because the reason that we start dating the rebound person is not that we find him really yummy, but that we are licking our wounds from a previous relationship. So, even though this rebound may be doomed, enjoy it while it lasts. And try not to hurt the other person, who may not be aware that this is your rebound relationship. That new person may be falling in love with you. Try not to lead him on too much because that can result in some serious and unnecessary guilt. Keep things light and fun. Make sure that you are both on the same page.

Woman Seeks Rebound Relationship

The following are some activities for finding a rebound relationship:

+ **Go to a bar.** Yes, it sounds obvious. Make eye contact with the man of your choice. Smile. If he smiles back, smile again, then look away. If you do this more than twice, and he does not make some excuse to come sit near you, then forget about it. If you keep smiling and making eye contact, he will probably come over eventually. Most men are sluts. The question is, do you want a slut?

+ **Go to a book reading.** You can strike up a conversation about the book.

+ **Go to an acting class.** Put the moves on your scene partner. Actors are horny.

Finding Mr. Perfect

The only person who should be dating Mr. Perfect is Miss Perfect. If you are not Miss Perfect, don't expect to find Mr. Perfect. No one is perfect. Perfection is too much to live up to. We are all imperfectly perfect in our own right. Rather than dream of Mr. Perfect, fantasize about the Lucky Man of the Future. Make a list of all the qualities you want in him. Write it down. Be very specific. The more specific, the better. Get creative. Include what he looks like, his habits, his hobbies, his job, the cute romantic things he does, and so on. This list will help you get excited about love again. Plus, in making the list, you're sending your wishes to your Higher Power. Put your list in your God box, then keep yourself open. Don't close yourself off to possibilities because you'll never know where Lucky Man of the Future will turn up.

So Where Is He?

Here are a few popular places to meet the next cowboy.

The Barfly

Meeting guys at a bar is probably the most popular choice for a few reasons. First, bars are designed for socializing.

Janice's Barfly Results

Most of the guys I dated I met in bars. Guess what. They were the types of guys that pick up girls in bars. Not good. Plus, they loved going to bars all the time. We could never have really meaningful conversations when all we did for fun was go to a bar and drink. My barfly experiences were not great.

Marni's Barfly Results

Bars are not on my list of fun places to go. I do not trust men who hit on women in bars. Dating-wise, I don't trust men who want to take me to a noisy bar for a date. A noisy bar is not a place to go if you want to be comfortable and get to know each other. Noisy bars are not conducive to deep and meaningful conversation; you just sit and drink. It is boring. I like to see things and go places.

They have the pool tables, the dance floor, and the strip (the path through the bar that people constantly walk). With so many socializing setups, you're bound to lock eyes with some stud. Second, at bars we can make believe. With liquid courage from a few Cosmopolitans, we become less shy . . . and the next day we can blame the alcohol. If you meet a guy at a bar, you have a very good chance of meeting the kind of guy who picks up girls in a bar . . . and possibly guys who seek out drunk girls to take advantage of. If you are still interested in him the next day, and he asks you out on a date, *make sure* your next date is sober. Then, you can accurately decide if you really like this guy or if it was the beer talking.

POWER TOOL

Fancy Hotel Bars

Take yourself out for tea to a fancy hotel bar. Choose an elegant hotel with an inspiring view of the city or the ocean. The kind of hotel with fireplaces in the lobby and tea for four dollars in a very fancy cup. They have a calm, classy ambiance, and you can't help but feel pampered. Plus, you never know who will come along and ask to join you for tea.

The Scholar

Picking up boys in class is an attractive option because you already have something in common to talk about. If you see a cute boy and are interested in getting to know him, sit near him. There may be a chance for in-class group activities, and you'll stand a better chance of being in his group if you sit near him. Sitting near him also opens up the option of casually asking him a question about homework, offering him a piece of gum, or asking him the time. A very nice bonus to picking up a boy in the

Janice's Scholar Results

In one class, I was put in a study group with a boy named Scott. I remarked to a friend that I was so lucky to be in Scott's study group because he was the cutest boy in the class. Throughout the semester, Scott and I talked and giggled uncontrollably. When the class was completed, Scott and I remained great friends. Eventually, he told me he was gay. I had suspected this for a while, but you have to let people tell you these things in their own time. I'm so glad I sat next to the cute boy in class. And I am so glad he was gay. I ended up with an amazing lifelong friend.

Marni's Scholar Results

Class is a wonderful place to meet boys and form crushes. I met someone wonderful in my acting class. There was no pressure to try to be cool because we were in class together, so we weren't worried about impressing anyone. We met under the pretense of just being ourselves and letting that shine through. Beware though, many actors, while emotionally available, have issues. Make sure your pick is working on himself.

classroom is that you can strategically leave class at the same time and strike up a conversation in the hallway.

The Coworker

Though there are many people who advise against mixing business and pleasure, picking someone up in the workplace is becoming increasingly common. Why? Because we spend the better part of our waking hours with the same coworkers day after day. Romantic sparks are bound to fly. If you begin developing a relationship with a coworker, be prepared to be grist for the rumor mill. Also, consider what will happen if you break up. You may have to see your ex on a daily basis, which could affect your job performance.

Other popular ways of meeting the next lucky guy include:

+ As a friend of a friend (a popular choice because the friend can give you details)
+ At a bookstore (Janice's personal favorite. Never actually happened but hope springs eternal)
+ At a coffee shop
+ Online
+ At the gym
+ At a house of worship
+ At a museum
+ At a party
+ At a diner counter (chat with everyone or chat with no one and read the paper)
+ At the grocery store (somewhere between the melons and bananas)

Janice's Coworker Results

I dated a guy at work. At first, it was great fun. Kissing in the elevator, meeting secretly in the lobby coffee shop, passing each other in the hall. We had decided to keep our romance a secret. It was hard not to react when someone would talk about him and his projects. Eventually, there were rumors about us. I even heard a rumor that he was dating a hot new girl. Dating at work was fun but very distracting. Eventually we broke up, but by then we were both at different companies, so I didn't have to deal with the awkwardness.

Marni's Running Partner

I have always fantasized about having a crush on a cute coworker, but alas, I've never had a cute coworker. Poor me. Instead, I ended up falling for my running partner. We would meet early in the morning, having just rolled out of bed with hair on my legs, hair on my tongue, and stubble under my arms. We would run in the breathtaking chilly morning air. Since we would sometimes run in silence, we were already comfortable with silences between us. We would talk about our week or what we were going to do that night. Eventually, I realized that not only did I enjoy talking to him but that he saw me looking my worst, and he still liked me. The fact that I knew I didn't have to do anything to impress him made me feel really comfortable being with him.

The First
Few
Minutes
With
Cowboy #2

During the first few minutes of meeting the love of the moment, our rose-colored bottle cap glasses are so thick that we can't see or think clearly. We are so out of the moment that we are out of our minds. We imagine:

+ How our first name would go with his last name

+ How the cowboy would look naked

+ How his hands would feel on our breasts

+ What trips we would go on together

All these fantasies are fun and totally acceptable. But remember that they are just fantasies. Try your best to stay real with your thoughts.

Stop Signs—Whoa, Slow This Horse Down

Often, we only see what we want to see, and we choose to ignore the things we don't want to see. Here are a few stop signs to keep in mind when you first start dating someone:

+ You're not physically attracted to him.

+ When you're making love, you'd rather be reading a magazine.

+ Your eyes glaze over when he talks.

+ You have nothing at all in common. You keep wondering what time it is.

+ He tells you things you don't agree with and you choose to ignore them.

+ You click your heels together and think, "There is no place like away from here."

+ Your gut is asking you why you are with this guy.

+ When you look at his package, you think, "Yuck, I don't want to ever come in contact with that thing!"

+ You find yourself wondering if he gets skid marks in his underwear.

+ After spending time with him you want to spend the rest of the day in bed ... alone.

+ You're excited he's taking you to a nice restaurant, but not because you're going with him.

+ If you know in your heart that if he wasn't paying for the meal, you'd rather be eating it with someone else.

+ You don't feel compelled to look at his package, or dare picture him on top of you.

+ You feel drained when you spend time with him.

+ You're relieved when he goes out of town.

+ You check your messages constantly while you're with him, wondering what you've been missing.

+ You start wondering what is in it for you.

+ He's a dick to his mom—definitely a stop sign. How he treats his mother is how he will eventually treat you.

+ The only good thing about this guy is his looks.

The First
Few
Minutes
With
Cowboy #2

155

Remember, men are sold "as is." You cannot change them. People only change when they want to change. Don't sign up to save him or teach him. It is not your job. Choose to be with him because you like being with him exactly how he is today. True love is loving him for who he is, not who he has the potential to be or what he can potentially do for you.

Listen to Your Gut

Instinct resides in your gut. Take a breath, unclench your toes, soften your tongue. You'll have a gut reaction with this new fella. Trust this instinctive reaction. If you really don't want to be with him, your gut will churn. Conversely, if you want to be with him, you may feel butterflies of joy. Trust your gut's reaction. Your body knows more than you realize.

Are You Lassoing the Same Cowboy Over and Over?

"We tend to repeat that which we have not yet worked out."

—*Sigmund Freud*

Yep, we do. We repeat the same relationship over and over again until its issues have been resolved. So, if you haven't fully evaluated and learned from your past relationship, you may be destined to have the same problems with this new relationship. Repetition is not necessarily a bad thing. We learn and we grow, and often that means that we have to repeat the same things over and over again until we learn that it may not work for us.

The Evolution of Man

When looking back at our collection of exes, it looks like a human evolution chart where the ape starts off dragging his knuckles and gradually becomes more and more upright until he's wearing a business suit and toting a briefcase. In this comparison, the first guys we date are of the Neanderthal era, where they use too much hair product, douse on the cologne, and are obsessed with touching our titties. As we continue to date, we learn what we want and what we don't want in a man. Our tastes

become more refined until at last our mate is completely upright and is, hopefully, wearing cute Calvin Klein undies.

The Stakes Get Higher as We Get Older

Along the way, dating becomes more serious and the stakes get higher because:

+ **Our biological clocks are ticking.** Facts are facts. We can't fight nature forever. If you want children, you have a limited window. Finding the father of your children isn't as much of a focus at age eighteen as it is at age thirty-eight.

+ **Pressure from family and friends to get married.** Although this shouldn't even be a consideration because you're the one who has to live with the groom, the constant nagging gets under your skin after a while.

+ **As we get older, the fish in the sea become more set in their ways.** They begin to do weird things like smell their underwear instead of just their socks, and their morning toilet time takes longer and longer.

+ **Cash.** As we get older, we begin to make real money that we just didn't have when we were in our early twenties. We move in together. We buy furniture together. We share custody of cats and dogs. We generally merge our lives more closely together than when we all lived with our parents, which makes it more complicated when we break up.

Dating
You
While
You're
Dating
Him

It feels exhilarating to be swept away by new romance. That said, being swept off your feet for too long can drain your system. At the beginning of a new romance, it is normal to be anxious and excited and psychotically happy whenever you are with him. Your body gets shaky and sweaty and may suddenly feel as if it has forgotten how to digest food. You go to sleep with a big smile on your face. Often, you don't even feel capable of calming down enough to fall asleep because this new romance is so great.

It is normal to have the desire, or feel the obligation, to give all of yourself to him. You could find yourself getting so swept up in the newness and excitement that you think to yourself, "So what if I don't get enough sleep or don't eat healthily or have a hang over tomorrow. I am in love tonight!" When we are with a new boy, nothing else matters except being with him. We think, "How lucky that I get to feel this good right now. I don't want to go to sleep or think about being tired in the morning." Your body is in excitement mode, and even though it feels wonderful, it can drain you.

Mamma's Boy

Many men are conditioned to be selfish and not even realize it. Most of them grew up with personal maids (a.k.a. their mothers). Moms enjoy serving their sons, hence their sons come to think that you will, too. If you should come upon one of these men, it is up to you to shine the light of reality into their fable.

Men want what they want, and they are going to try and get it no matter what. Most will even convince themselves that they are going about it in the most honorable way possible. When he does something, such as not caring if something is going to make you stressed or not caring about your personal needs, it is not really about him not caring about *you*. You don't even come into play. Your needs don't even pass through his consciousness. He's thinking of himself.

Take Care of Yourself First

If you sacrifice your needs at the start of a relationship, you set yourself up to be pissed off if the relationship doesn't meet your expectations. Here are some simple reminders about keeping your head on your shoulders while you fall head over heels for him.

Sleep

You may not want to pry yourself away from him Sunday night when you are cuddling together. However, if you have work Monday morning and you know that you won't get

Marni's Mamma's Boys

I've dated plenty of men in this category, and I've finally learned something. Men always take care of themselves first. You need not worry about them; you need to worry about you and what will make you happy. Women are used to taking care of others first, but what we need to do is take care of ourselves before anyone else.

your best sleep in the same bed with him, then it is up to you to get yourself home and into your own bed. If he doesn't have to be up early the next morning, he is going to try and keep you in that bed until you physically stand up and put on your shoes. It's hard to get up and leave. We all want to stay and feel like we are being loved and taken care of. Remember, men take care of themselves first, so you need to do the same. Taking care of yourself in this way is the most loving thing that you can do for yourself. Fight to stay who you are. Keep your sleep routine. Nourish yourself in the way that works best for you. Take notes from the men in your life. That's what they do. They take care of themselves first.

Sometimes the most loving thing for ourselves is to be our own parent and get ourselves to bed.

Sex

Contrary to all that we like to believe about modern men and women being more like "partners" than polar opposites, it is the women's job to call the shots when it comes to stopping. Most men will keep pushing for more until you say, "stop." Not because they are bad guys or selfish or uncaring, but because, as my dad always told me, "Marni, a stiff prick has no conscience." Men do not always think with their brains. The most enlightened men out there, if faced with the possibility of sex, will trip over their face to get to it. Men will do or say anything to have sex with you. It can be hard to grasp this concept. Grasp it. They are animals. It's their instinct to spread as much of their DNA as possible. Cowgirls call the shots when it comes to stopping.

Food

You have to keep eating in a loving way for your body. Don't start eating pizza just because that is what you eat with him. Chances are, when you eat out, he will ask you what kind of food you want. He will be trying to be gracious. A gentleman knows it is part of his job to be gracious and ask you what you want. Then, you might do the same thing and say, "I don't care; what kind of food do you want?" Then you end up eating the crappy food he chooses instead of the chicken salad you knew your body was hoping for.

Do you hate Chinese food because it is too greasy? Are you a vegetarian and don't want to go to a steak house? Are you trying not to eat a lot of carbs and thus, don't want to go to an Italian restaurant with amazing bread on the table? If these are things that might bother you, or if overeating might cause you to be less in the moment with him and mad at yourself later, then don't set yourself up by going to a place where you know you won't be happy with the food. If you are going to want fish and vegetables or a chicken salad or a tofu burger, then think of a place that will have these things and tell him you want to go there instead. Stand up for yourself. He can go to his greasy spoon on his own time.

Insist on Getting What You Need and Want Even If You Are Scared

If you feel uncomfortable asking for what you want, get over it. Take a deep breath and ask for help from the universe. Ask for the strength to be both honest and kind. Then, leave the whole situation in the hands of your Higher Power.

Exercise

If you start putting your physical well-being second to his, sooner or later you will resent him. If you don't take care of yourself, you're going to get tired of the relationship fast. You'll blame him for your crankiness, your flabby body, the fact that you never see your friends, and so on. So keep your routines and take care of yourself.

Okay, this is the last time we're going to say it. If you want to keep him, take care of yourself first. It is absolutely, 100 percent, your job to take care of yourself, not his. Always put yourself before any man and any relationship. Putting yourself first is not selfish, it is smart. *Anything* you put before loving yourself you will eventually lose.

Keep from Sliding off the Saddle

When we're in a new relationship, it's fun to be swept off our feet. Even healthy. But at some point, we have to get back down to earth and look after ourselves. It's simply too wearing on our body, spirit, and mind if we stop looking after our own needs when we start dating someone new. To keep from sliding off the saddle:

+ Keep your routine.

+ Pray and meditate, even if it is just for a couple of minutes in the shower. This will help you check in with yourself.

+ Eat three balanced meals every day. No skimping.

+ Don't consume too many stimulants (cigarettes, sugar, and caffeine). They are toxins that put unnecessary stress on your body.

+ Get enough sleep.

+ Be vigilant about keeping your head in the present moment.

+ Schedule some time for just yourself every day.

POWER TOOL
Find Faith

Find and instill in yourself some sort of faith in a universal power greater than yourself that you believe loves you unconditionally and is taking care of you. Believe that this power will never give you anything that you can't handle. If you don't believe in this power, ask for the willingness to believe. Ask out loud if you have to.

Saving time just for you every day is imperative. If you don't save some of you for you, you will soon find yourself consumed by him. Fill yourself with you before you see him, or else it will be too easy to let yourself be filled with him, and then you'll feel empty when you're not with him. Don't let him be your everything. Don't let him be more important than you.

Keep A Connection to Your Cowgirl Friends

They are your lifeline. Though we'd hate to admit it, we've all stopped hanging out with our girlfriends when a cowboy came strutting through the door. Chances are, the cowgirls will be around a lot longer than the cowboys, so treat them right. They are your support group, your chosen family, your *amigas.* Don't diss them or they'll be saying *adios* if the next cowboy rides off into the sunset without you.

Congratulations!

You are on the path to healing and are becoming a stronger person! From this day forward, go out into the world with confidence, energy, and a heaping spoonful of spirituality. You are bold. You are brave. There is no one in the world who is exactly like you are! Congratulations.

To Our Readers

Conari Press, an imprint of Red Wheel/Weiser, publishes books on topics ranging from spirituality, personal growth, and relationships to women's issues, parenting, and social issues. Our mission is to publish quality books that will make a difference in people's lives—how we feel about ourselves and how we relate to one another. We value integrity, compassion, and receptivity, both in the books we publish and in the way we do business.

Our readers are our most important resource, and we value your input, suggestions, and ideas about what you would like to see published. Please feel free to contact us, to request our latest book catalog, or to be added to our mailing list.

Conari Press
An imprint of Red Wheel/Weiser, LLC
P.O. Box 612
York Beach, ME 03910-0612
www.conari.com

About the Authors

Marni Kamins and Janice MacLeod came together to write *The Breakup Repair Kit* over tea, trail mix, and two broken hearts. Marni holds a Master's degree in Spiritual Psychology, and Janice is an advertising copywriter. They both live in southern California. Visit them at *www.breakuprepairkit.com*.

Photograph by Meredith Kaplan